Managing Performance in the Public Sector

Second edition

Hans de Bruijn

Routledge
Taylor & Francis Group

LONDON AND NEW YORK

First published 2007
by Routledge
2 Park Square, Milton Park, Abingdon, Oxon OX14 4RN

Simultaneously published in the USA and Canada
by Routledge
270 Madison Ave, New York, NY 10016

Reprinted 2007

Routledge is an imprint of the Taylor & Francis Group, an informa business

© 2007 Hans de Bruijn

Typeset in Sabon and Gill Sans by
Graphicraft Ltd, Hong Kong
Printed and bound in Great Britain by
TJ International Ltd, Padstow, Cornwall

British Library Cataloguing in Publication Data
A catalogue record for this book is available from the British Library

Library of Congress Cataloging in Publication Data
Bruijn, J. A. de, 1962–
Managing performance in the public sector / Hans de Bruijn. – 2nd ed.
    p. cm.
    Includes bibliographical references and index.
    ISBN 0-415-40319-7 (hard cover) – ISBN 0-415-40320-0 (soft cover)
1. Public administration–Evaluation.   2. Organizational
effectiveness–Evaluation.   I. Title.

JF1338.A2B7813 2006
352.3'75–dc22
                                                        2006020183

ISBN10: 0-415-40319-7 (hbk)
ISBN10: 0-415-40320-0 (pbk)

ISBN13: 978-0-415-40319-1 (hbk)
ISBN13: 978-0-415-40320-7 (pbk)

Contents

Illustrations

Part I

Chapter I

An introduction to performance measurement

The beneficial effect of performance measurement

I Introduction and outline of the argument in this book

In recent years, management techniques from the private sector have penetrated deep into professional public sector organizations such as hospitals, universities, courts and schools. One of these techniques is performance management. The idea is that these professional organizations, like companies, provide products and services and that their performance – their output – can be measured. A court can be assessed by the number of judgements it passes, a police force by the number of fixed penalty notices it issues and scientists by the number of publications in scientific journals. A professional organization that manages to define its products can demonstrate its performance, which may improve its effectiveness, efficiency and legitimacy.[1]

A fruitless debate: public profession versus accountability

It is remarkable that positions are easily taken in the debate about performance measurement in the public sector. On the one hand, there is the view that performance measurement does not do any justice to the nature of the activities performed by professional organizations. Professional organizations are organizations that provide public services. These public services are multiple-value ones (i.e. they have to take several values into account) and are rendered in co-production (in cooperation with third parties). A school must make its pupils perform well, but must also have a good educational climate (multiple value); its pupils' performance depends on the school's effort, but also on the extent to which pupils are stimulated at home (co-production). A court must pass judgement as soon as possible, but its judgement must be well-considered (multiple value); a court can hardly influence the number of cases it has to deal with and the behaviour of the litigating parties (cooperation). Performance measurement reduces this complexity to one single dimension.

A manager who imposes output targets on a professional organization and is later pleased to find that they have been achieved is fooling himself. The example of the Soviet Union's centrally planned economy is often cited. Order a factory to make as many nails as possible from a given quantity of steel, and it will indeed produce many, lightweight, nails. Order the same factory to produce a certain weight in nails, given a certain quantity of steel, and the nails will be made as heavy as possible. In such a system, the professional question of whether the nails produced are functional is never asked. Something similar applies to professional organizations. In many cases it may not be difficult to achieve a certain output, so long as an organization is prepared to ignore professional considerations. Achieving output targets does not tell us anything about the professionalism and/or quality of the performance; an effort to reach output targets may even harm professionalism and quality.

The opposite view begins with the idea of accountability. The more complex the services that professional organizations must provide, the more necessary it is to grant these organizations autonomy in producing such services. While they are autonomous, they are also accountable, however: How do they spend public funds? Does society receive 'value for money'? After all, granting autonomy to a professional organization may cause it to develop an internal orientation, to be insufficiently client-oriented, to develop excessive bureaucracy and therefore to underperform. Autonomy without accountability conceals both good and bad performance. Moreover, if organizations are accountable, they can learn from each other. The poorly performing organizations might notice what the well-performing professional organizations are and might subsequently introduce their best practices.

Accountability is a form of communication and requires the information that professional organizations have available to be reduced and aggregated. Performance measurement is a very powerful communication tool: it reduces the complex performance of a professional organization to its essence. It therefore makes it possible to detect poor performance, allowing an organization to be corrected if it performs poorly. If a professional organization performs well, performance measurement might play an important role in making this transparent and in acquiring legitimacy.

Both lines of reasoning are rooted in the same development: the need to grant autonomy to professionals performing complex public tasks. On the one hand, this development implies that professionals account for their performance: autonomy and accountability go hand in hand. On the other hand, it implies that it is becoming increasingly difficult to define performance, since autonomy is necessary because the performance is so complex.

This shows that the antithesis set out above is fruitless: both lines of reasoning are correct. Therefore, an important question in this book is whether it is possible to develop a more balanced perspective on performance measurement. Is it possible to design performance measurement in such a way that it takes into account both the complexity of the profession and the need for accountability?

An outline of the argument in this book

I intend to develop this more balanced perspective by means of an argument that will proceed as follows:

- First, I indicate that performance measurement can have a beneficial effect on professional organizations. It may improve the professionalism of the service rendered, the professional organization's innovative power and the quality of (political) decision-making. Negative judgements about performance measurement tend to be passed too soon; performance measurement is a much more differentiated activity than is often suggested (this chapter).
- In addition, strong criticism may be levelled against performance measurement. Performance measurement has a great many perverse effects: it may bureaucratize an organization, killing all incentives for professionalism and innovation and causing performance measurement to lead mainly to strategic behaviour. Performance measurement may considerably widen the gap between political decision-making and implementation (Chapter 2).
- Then there is the question about the dynamics of performance measurement systems. How do they develop in the course of time? I summarize this dynamism in five laws, the most important of which is the Law of Decreasing Effectiveness (Chapter 3).
- This gives rise to an ambiguous picture: apart from the beneficial effects of performance measurement, there are perverse effects. This raises the question as to how performance measurement can be designed so as to minimize the perverse effects. For this purpose, in Chapter 4 I introduce three criteria that performance measurement should meet if it is to fulfil its function properly: interaction, variety and dynamics. These criteria may be used to design a system of performance measurement. This is why I refer to them as 'design principles'. I work out these design principles in Chapters 5 to 7.
- Chapter 5 focuses on the question of how performance measurement can be *trustful*. This means that both management and professionals have confidence in a system of performance measurement. The answer

is that a system of performance measurement should be developed in *interaction* between management and professionals. Applying performance measurement also requires such cooperation.

- Chapter 6 deals with creating *rich pictures* of a professional performance. For management as well as for professionals, performance measurement should take the multiplicity of professional activities into account and not degenerate into a single activity. This is why performance measurement should always tolerate *variety* (in product definitions, for example, or performance indicators, interpretations of output targets).

- Closely associated with this is the idea of *lively* performance measurement. Performance measurement must be an activity that gives rise to management and professionals feeling challenged. I explain in Chapter 7 that this liveliness can only be created if performance measurement focuses not only on professionals' products, but also on the process of generating them. Performance measurement should not confine itself to paying attention to numbers of judgements, official police reports or scientific articles. It should also pay attention to administering justice, fighting crime and conducting research. These illustrations imply that, apart from a product approach, there is a need for a *process approach*. Liveliness also requires a system of performance measurement to be *dynamic*: it should adapt itself to changing conditions.

- Finally, in Chapter 8, I summarize the findings of this book about the significance which performance measurement may have in professional organizations.

Focus and terminology

Performance measurement is used in many organizations. In this book, I deal mainly with public professional organizations, examples of which may be conventional professional organizations such as hospitals, universities and the court service, but also many 'street-level' organizations such as the police, the probation service and a large number of departmental implementing bodies.

For the sake of readability, I consistently use the terms 'management', 'manager' and 'professional/professionals' in this book. The professional is the person who designs the primary process; the manager is the person who, by performance measurement among other methods, tries to steer this process and is responsible for it in most cases. It should be remembered here that the same player can fill both roles because many professional organizations are multi-layer organizations. Take, for example, a court. The

Minister of Justice is a managerial player and may regard the Council for the Judiciary – many European countries have such a Council – as a representative of the profession. This may be different from the perspective of a court: the court represents the profession; the Council represents the managerial system. An individual judge may take yet another view: he or she is the professional; the court management is the managerial player. Something similar is true of the layered structure of national systems of universities: the Ministry of Education, the Executive Board of a university, the Dean of a faculty, the faculty's research groups and individual researchers; or of the layers formed by the Ministry of Health, the Executive Board of a hospital, the management of a division and individual surgeons.

Who is the manager and who is the professional may therefore differ from echelon to echelon. This conclusion is relevant to the question of how the performance measurement systems between these layers relate to each other (Chapter 6).

In this chapter, I first give a brief description of performance measurement (Section 2). I then go on to discuss the positive effects of performance measurement (Sections 3–6). Next, I deal with a number of objections to performance measurement (Section 7).

2 Performance measurement: what it is and its functions

In this section, I set out – very briefly – how performance measurement is defined in the literature and what functions it may have. For more detailed considerations of these introductory questions, I refer the reader to the literature.[2]

The central idea behind performance measurement is a simple one: a professional organization formulates its envisaged performance and indicates how this performance may be measured by defining performance indicators. Once the organization has performed its tasks, it may be shown whether the envisaged performance was achieved and how much it cost.

The problem here is, of course, that the effects of an organization are often difficult to measure. This is because public performance has to take multiple values into account and is achieved in co-production. Furthermore, the period between an intervention and its final, envisaged effect may be lengthy. This makes it impossible in many cases to measure the final effect of a professional (the 'outcome'), not least when abstract goals such as liveability, safety, integration or quality are involved. What is measurable is the direct effects of interventions by an organization (the 'output': the licence issued, the fixed penalty notice, the article published), while, in some cases – somewhere between direct effects and final effects – intermediate effects may be identified which are also measurable. It should be pointed out that the terminology in the literature is not always unambiguous. Some writers give the concept 'output' a very narrow definition (only the direct effects), while others use a very broad definition (including the outcome).[3] In this book, I confine the meaning of performance measurement to the effects that are measurable. This choice seems legitimate to me because it matches much of the everyday language used in organizations: many organizations that use performance measurement count the products they generate.[4] Concepts such as 'output' or 'product measurement' may be regarded as synonymous with performance measurement.

Once a professional organization has defined its products, it can plan the volume of its output over a certain period and establish at the end of this period what output was achieved. As a result, a professional organization – like many organizations in the private sector – may pass through a planning cycle, in which performance is planned, achieved and measured. This is often accompanied by a strong orientation on goals. Performance measurement forces an organization to formulate targets for the various programmes for which it is responsible and to state the period within which they must be achieved. It will then show its ambitions for each of these targets in performance indicators.

Performance measurement can then fulfil a number of functions.[5] Those mentioned most frequently are the following:

- *Creating transparency*. Performance measurement leads to transparency and can thus play a role in accountability processes. An organization can make clear what products it provides and – by means of an input–output analysis – what costs are involved.
- *Learning*. An organization takes a step further when it uses performance measurement to learn. Thanks to the transparency created, an organization can learn what it does well and where improvements are possible.
- *Appraising*. A performance-based appraisal may now be given (by the management of the organization, by third parties) about an organization's performance.
- *Sanctioning*. Finally, appraisal may be followed by a positive sanction when performance is good, or by a negative sanction when performance is insufficient. The sanction may be a financial one, but other types of sanction are possible.

These functions have an ascending degree of compulsion: the impact of transparency will be limited, the impact of a sanction can be very high. Each of these functions can apply to an organization, but also facilitate comparison – a 'benchmark' – between organizations.

The beneficial effect of performance measurement

In the literature, a great deal of research is available about performance measurement. A first impression is that performance measurement has a beneficial effect.

3 Performance measurement leads to transparency and is therefore an incentive for innovation

First, performance measurement leads to transparency. This transparency has both an internal and an external function.

The internal function

A professional public sector organization has limited external incentives for effectiveness and efficiency, and therefore has an almost natural tendency to develop 'red tape': for example, dysfunctional procedures, discussions on structures, too much support staff. This has been beautifully formulated in Parkinson's Law: an increase in employees leads to a reinforced increase in loss of time because internal, non-productive tasks become more voluminous.[6]

The result of this may be that for many activities in an organization it is unclear what they contribute to the primary process and thus to the organization's right of existence. For such an organization to formulate its products and then to meet its performance targets creates transparency, which is an incentive for innovation in the organization. An internal discussion may be started, for example, about how much various types of activities contribute to the organization's performance. There is also a clear standard for appraising new procedures, new structures or new support staff: How much do they contribute to improving the organization's performance?[7]

Suppose, for example, that the funding of a court is made dependent on the number of judgements delivered. Courts have two types of legal professionals: judges and legally trained support staff. Performance measurement may be an incentive to review the existing division of tasks between judges and support staff critically. If a judgement brings in money, the logical question would be what a judgement costs.

The next question is whether a more efficient division of tasks between judges and support staff is possible. What activities can be performed by the cheap staff and what activities by the expensive judges? Is it desirable for an expensive judge to perform activities that a cheap support staff member can also perform? Performance measurement is thus an incentive to review an existing practice. Performance measurement rationalizes and leads to innovations.

'What gets measured gets done'[8] summarizes arguments of this kind: an organization that can make its performance visible has goals on which it can focus, and this visibility will tend to be an automatic incentive to improve its performance.

The external function

In many Western countries, 'quality of life' issues are high on the political agenda. People want good education, a safe neighbourhood, health care without waiting lists and correct treatment by the courts. Whereas mainly macro-issues were on the political agenda until the 1980s – a fair distribution of income, peace and security, the position of the Third World – many micro-issues that manifest themselves in people's immediate surroundings are now also on the agenda. This means that people call politicians to account about the service provided by, for example, the police, schools, hospitals and courts. In turn, politicians will call these professional organizations to account about the service provided. Measuring performance is an elegant way of calling an organization to account: it reduces performance, complex as it tends to be, to a number of figures that are easy to communicate.

Police organizations measure crime trends and clear-up rates. The New York Police Department, for example, has highly detailed statistics that are constantly updated and posted on the internet. The public can see the crime trends for their own particular neighbourhood. Good figures may boost the authority of the police organization; poor figures can stimulate awareness that change and improvement are needed.

4 Performance measurement rewards performance and prevents bureaucracy

A second cluster of arguments is based on the opposite reasoning: performance measurement is a form of output steering and is desirable, because input and throughput steering are a disincentive for performance.

Input steering particularly rewards the planning and formulating of goals and intentions. It is often an incentive to formulate goals and intentions to be as ambitious as possible, since one organization distinguishes itself from another by being ambitious. Input steering also leads to a *claim culture*. Plans compete for scarce resources, so there is an incentive to claim a maximum of funds. There is also a matching form of strategic behaviour: finding out what the manager's interests and preferences are and formulating goals in such a way that they match these interests and preferences.

Throughput steering concentrates on the processes and activities within an organization and not on their results. Researchers are not rewarded on the basis of their scientific production (output), or on the basis of their plans (input), but on the basis of the time they spend on research. Throughput steering leads to an *expense account culture*. It is attractive to work as many hours as possible. It is an 'incentive' for internal activities and a 'disincentive' for performance.

> An example is that of a nursing home in Illinois steered on throughput (the number of bedridden patients). The nursing home thus had a strong incentive to keep patients in bed rather than an incentive for quality of care (including getting patients up and about again as soon as possible).[9]

Evidently, throughput steering also gives rise to its own strategic behaviour: intensification of the number of internal actions which do not improve eventual performance. The more hours researchers need for publishing an article, the more they are rewarded.

Output steering concentrates on products and is thus an incentive to be productive: neither the good intention (input) nor the diligent effort (throughput), but the result is rewarded.

> Research conducted at my own university shows, for example, that the introduction of an output model for the allocation of budgets has led to a rise in the number of scientific publications: a rise of 50 per cent in total over a three-year period, in spite of a 5 per cent fall in numbers of scientific staff.[10] Other professional organizations, too, report a link between the introduction of performance measurement and an increase in output; for example, in municipalities[11] and in higher education.[12]

Performance measurement also helps to de-bureaucratize an organization. It allows an organization to invest less in making plans (input) or time-keeping systems (throughput). Moreover, organizations that perform well tend to be 'rewarded' with autonomy, because there is far less need for a manager to intervene in a well-performing organization than in a poorly performing organization. If an organization performs well, plans or timekeeping systems are less necessary.

5 Performance measurement promotes learning

The third advantage of performance measurement is that it may promote learning processes both between and within organizations.

Between organizations

Figures pre-eminently lend themselves to comparison: between police forces, schools, hospitals, courts and so on. Differences between professional organizations may be a reason to identify *best practices*: methods that evidently bring better performance. Comparison may also be an incentive for learning, because it may create *problem awareness*. The board of a university with a low ranking or a city that scores low in a safety monitor may use this score to drive learning and change processes. The communicative power of figures is thus used to create a *sense of urgency*: the university or the city has a major problem, so action is called for.

Within organizations

An important characteristic of professional organizations is the non-intervention principle: professionals do not intervene in each other's domain and thus leave the fellow professional alone.[13] Non-intervention may harm professional organizations because it hampers the learning processes: professionals receive insufficient feedback on their performance. Performance measurement may play a role in breaking this non-intervention principle. Output figures make the differences between professional units clear and offer management the opportunity to ask the units questions about these differences. What explains the difference? Why is one unit able to produce more than another unit with the same resources? Output figures also make the differences between professionals visible, at least more visible than in a non-intervention culture, and may be a reason for professionals to start asking each other questions. Output figures may thus be an incentive for learning processes.

The New York police system of performance measurement produces figures on a neighbourhood level, which makes it an important trigger for professional interaction. The figures are a reason for police officials to ask each other critical questions in meetings specially convened for this purpose: about crime trends, about the explanations for them, about the actions colleagues take when crime levels rise and about the effectiveness of these actions. Participants in these meetings tend to ask each other tough questions: police officials are 'peppered with questions'.[14] This results in learning processes. Performance measurement empowers because it is a driver for police organizations to constantly subject their own strategies to critical review.

6 Performance measurement enhances intelligence

In the fourth place, performance measurement yields information that may be used to improve the professional service provision.

Measuring crime by neighbourhood allows crime trends to be made visible. Which offences are rising in volume and which are falling? How does crime move across the city? Does the introduction of a zero-tolerance strategy in a neighbourhood cause crime to shift to other neighbourhoods – the balloon effect?

Therefore, output figures may also be used to improve an organization's intelligence. This intelligence is also important because many professional organizations are interdependent for their own output. In the criminal proceedings chain, for example, the police output strongly influences the output of the Public Prosecution Service. A police organization that can furnish clarity about its output (both on long-term trends and providing short-term, 'real time' information) enables the Public Prosecution Service to improve the forecast of its input, thereby improving the arrangement of its production process. Something similar is true of the relationship between the Public Prosecution Service and the courts: the output of the one is the input of the other.

7 Objections to performance measurement

It is not so difficult to raise a number of objections to the idea that a professional organization generates measurable products. This section

Table 1.1 Conditions under which performance measurement is possible and problematic

Type 1 products: Performance measurement possible	Type 2 products: Performance measurement problematic
Products are single value	Products are multiple value
An organization is product-oriented	An organization is process-oriented
Autonomous production	Co-production: products are generated together with others
Products are isolated	Products are interwoven
Causalities are known	Causalities are unknown
Quality definable in performance indicators	Quality not definable in performance indicators
Uniform products	Variety of products
Environment is stable	Environment is dynamic

examines a number of frequently raised objections, represented in Table 1.1.[15] I would like to point out, however, that this enumeration is not intended to show that performance measurement is impossible, but to problematize the overly simple use of performance measurement.

Multiple-value, not single-value products

Products are multiple-value when they have to take account of a number of different values which may also conflict. In Section 1, I already mentioned the examples of the school and the court. Performance measurement carries the risk of a manager ignoring some of these values (it only meets clearly definable and quantifiable performance goals) and therefore does not present a proper picture of a professional's performance.

Process-oriented, not product-oriented

Many public organizations are highly process-oriented. Organizations which make policies in an environment that comprises many parties will invest heavily in consultations and negotiations with these parties. The outcome of such negotiations may be difficult to predict; a good process of interaction may nevertheless yield disappointing products. Something similar applies to situations of uncertainty. Take research institutes: the products of innovative research are difficult to predict. A well-devised and well-performed research *process* may nevertheless yield limited results but no products such as articles in scientific journals. When processes dominate, performance measurement is pointless.

Products are produced together with others; the professional is not an autonomous producer

The performance of many professional organizations is relational: it is achieved in co-production with third parties. The duration of criminal proceedings before a court depends partly on the stance taken by the defence counsel; a school's performance depends partly on the attitude of the parents.

Consequently, performance resulting from co-production may only partly be ascribed to professional organizations. Performance measurement is based on the idea of an organization being an autonomous producer. Many systems of performance measurement wrongly link the performance achieved and measured to a professional's effort, which produces an incorrect picture.

Products are interwoven, not isolated

Products of professional organizations may interfere with one another. The performance of a municipality's spatial planning department may affect the municipality's environmental performance. When a spatial planning department is measured chiefly in terms of its own products, it has no incentive to invest in good coordination with the environment department. An individual organization scoring high on its own indicators may therefore harm the collective performance. Performance measurement may thus reinforce existing compartmentalization within an organization or between organizations. It might be a disincentive for joined-up government.

Causalities are unknown or 'contested', not objective

The relationship between effort and result is not always known. The interview with a prisoner, aimed at preventing recidivism, is just one of the factors determining whether or not he or she will reoffend. Where such causalities are unknown or contested, there may be either one of two consequences. The outcome (in the example: no recidivism) is only partly the result of the effort made, which means that the measurement does not produce an adequate picture of the performance of the organization concerned. Alternatively, the organization may respond by choosing to formulate output indicators (the number of interviews conducted, for example), but these, too, provide no adequate picture of the organization's performance.

Quality measurement requires a rich picture, performance measurement leads to a poor picture

Sometimes it is possible to incorporate quality into a performance indicator. Take the number of scientific articles published by a researcher. Many journals have an impact factor, which says something about the quality of a particular journal. Those who publish frequently in a journal with a high impact factor will not only earn a high quantitative score, but will probably also deliver high-quality research. Performance measurement will then be less problematic. However, the quality of a great deal of a professional's performance is difficult to establish with the help of performance indicators. The number of a court's judgements says nothing about the quality of those judgements. If performance measurement is nevertheless used, there is a risk that attention paid to quantity will drive out attention paid to quality.

Even the same type of performance shows variety, not uniformity

The same performance may have different meaning in different contexts. A faculty's performance includes its international, scientific publications. In a diffuse field such as business administration, with a fragmented scientific community and a tradition of pluralism, acceptance of a publication means something different from acceptance in a clearly delineated field such as theoretical physics, with a close-knit scientific community and an unambiguous language. If the same product can have a totally different meaning in different contexts, performance measurement will present an incorrect picture of reality. Performance measurement will then invite comparison of types of performance that are incomparable in principle.

The environment is dynamic, not static

Some of the above objections become even more serious when an organization's environment is dynamic. When the behaviour of the co-producers in a professional organization continually changes or when 'quality' is redefined, the possibilities for good performance measurement will decrease. The possibilities to compare performance over a certain time will also decrease. Performance measurement is based on the tacit assumption that the environment of professional organizations is stable.

Chapter 2

The perverse effects of performance measurement

1 Introduction

The positive effects of performance measurement were discussed in Chapter 1. Performance measurement promotes transparency and innovation, it is an incentive to be productive, may help to de-bureaucratize an organization, promotes learning and may enhance an organization's intelligence position. There is another picture, however, apart from this beneficial effect of performance measurement: performance measurement creates a large number of perverse effects. I shall outline these effects in this chapter (Sections 2–8) and I give an initial explanation for them (Section 9). In Chapter 3, I discuss the dynamics of performance measurement: what effects will manifest themselves in the long term?

2 Performance measurement is an incentive for strategic behaviour

Performance measurement may be an important stimulus to a professional organization's productivity. This is because the organization's output will at least be made visible, and it may also be rewarded for it.

There is another picture, however: measuring and rewarding products may be an incentive for strategic behaviour. A professional organization increases its output in accordance with the system's criteria, but this increase in output has no significance or has a negative significance from a professional perspective. This form of strategic behaviour is sometimes referred to as 'gaming the numbers'.[1]

Here are a number of examples:

- The output figures of the Dutch Public Prosecution Service show that it drops considerably fewer cases than in the preceding years. A reduction in the number of cases dropped is one of the goals of the Minister of Justice;

the service that succeeds in reducing the number of cases dropped will receive a bonus. So this is a successful form of performance measurement. Actually, a Public Prosecution Service employee already deletes a large number of offences from the computer at the police station, thereby reducing the number of cases that reach the Public Prosecution Service, which partly accounts for the positive figure mentioned above. The numbers are thus reduced artificially, qualifying the Public Prosecution Service for the financial bonus awarded by the Minister.[2]

- One performance indicator for the American FBI is the number of arrests. A constant increase in the performance required by politicians invites strategic behaviour. The FBI proves capable of reaching ever higher output figures as regards arrests by arresting deserters from the armed forces. They are easier to detect than other lawbreakers. These arrests serve hardly any social interest at all and are only made to meet the performance standards. As a result, the percentage of detainees that is actually prosecuted is extremely low.[3]

- A particular department in the Australian army is responsible for housing servicemen stationed far from home. After a first interview, the unit makes the serviceman in question an offer as soon as possible. When he declines the offer, the unit registers his reasons and makes a second offer. This procedure is repeated when he declines again. In order to improve the performance of this unit, a new performance indicator is defined: the percentage of servicemen accepting a house after a maximum of three offers should be improved. This percentage turns out to be 100 per cent in less than no time. The explanation is simple: the unit introduces the phenomenon of an 'informal offer' and does not make a formal offer until it is certain that it will be accepted.[4]

- The world of health care also contains numerous examples of 'gaming the numbers'. British hospitals have long waiting times at Accident and Emergency departments, and various governments have tried to reduce them. In the week when it is measured whether waiting times have actually been reduced, hospitals double their staff to reach the best possible score in the measuring system. Other strategies: patients have to stay in the ambulance because only the waiting time in the hospital counts; those who go from the waiting room to the department and have to wait there in the corridor no longer count as waiting patients because they are in the department. Another example is the introduction of 'hello nurses'. Hospitals that manage to reduce the time between an admission and the start of treatment receive a financial reward. Many hospitals prove able to do so. The explanation is simple: a nurse visits the patients immediately after their admission, telling them that their treatment has started, and then ticks this on a form: the 'hello nurse'.[5]

There is strategic behaviour here because the performance in these examples only exists on paper. The performance on paper has no social significance or only a very limited one. Incidentally, this strategic behaviour may be evaluated in very different ways: from an innocent form of creative accounting to fraud.

3 Performance measurement blocks innovation

An organization faced with performance measurement will make an effort to optimize its production process, allowing it to achieve its output as efficiently as possible, particularly when performance measurement is linked to some form of financial reward. This may be a strong incentive to think in 'cash cows': what products are relatively easy to make, enabling as much money as possible to be generated?

Thinking in cash cows means that an organization minimizes its throughput, nearly always at the expense of *innovation*. Anyone wishing to innovate will have to explore the unknown and accept the risk that the results may be either what was expected or less than expected. Innovation may therefore harm an organization's output. Performance measurement rewards the constant reproduction of the existing practices.[6]

> An example of this is a research group on public finance within a university. The researchers have specialized in research into levies for a number of years. They have acquired considerable expertise in the subject and are able to publish articles about the subject relatively quickly and simply, both in national and international journals. The system of performance measurement rewards them richly for it.[7]

4 Performance measurement blocks ambition

The phenomenon that organizations raise their performance by optimizing their input is also well known. The selection criterion for input is that it demands the lowest possible throughput to obtain the desired output. Empirical research also reveals this form of behaviour, known as 'creaming' or 'cherry-picking'.

> • Schools that are rewarded for performance (laid down in a 'charter' between the funding authority and the school's management) or for functioning in a 'voucher system' (spending the vouchers depends partly on the school's performance) have been found to select their input. They manage to keep out potential pupils with learning or behavioural problems or successfully use a 'counselling out' strategy.[8] The school's performance thus goes up, rendering

the agreements in the charter easier to meet or improving the chances that parents will opt for this school. As a result, the variety of the pupil population within schools will fall below an educationally desirable level.[9]

- An example too delightful to omit: the fight against muskrats can be based on a bonus system. People receive a certain amount of money for every dead muskrat they catch and hand in. This performance is included in many Dutch municipal performance surveys. Catching muskrats is important in the Low Countries because they damage the dikes, which increases vulnerability to flooding. Here, too, the phenomenon of input optimization occurs. Rats are normally caught in winter, before they build a nest and bear young. Once a performance reward has been introduced, it becomes attractive to allow father and mother muskrat to start a family first. 'Why should you catch two rats in winter, if there might be thirty of them in spring, parents and offspring together?'[10]

An organization optimizing its input does so at the expense of its *ambitions*. An organization needs to put in less effort to achieve a desirable output if it manipulates the quality or quantity of the input.

5 Performance measurement veils actual performance

Performance measurement serves to allow an organization to account for its performance and is an important tool to slightly objectify its (public) account. It enables non-professional actors (e.g. managers, boards, ministers or Parliament) to penetrate the capillaries of an organization.

However, performance measurement may also veil an organization's performance. The higher the extent to which information is aggregated, the remoter it is from the primary process where it was generated. Consequently, insight may be lost into the causal connections between effort and performance that exist on the level of the primary process (and give a meaning to the figures). Non-professional actors see only the aggregated data and run the risk of construing their own causalities from them.[11] In other words, performance measurement casts a veil.

It may be added that the output figure which produces a picture on the level of the whole (macro) is always an average and therefore cannot simply be applied to the individual parts (micro) that have provided information for this aggregated picture. If conclusions are nevertheless construed on the basis of the aggregated data, or if macro-pictures are directly translated to the micro-level, the risk is that injustice will be done to performance.

A scientist published an article about the swimming behaviour of dolphins in an international biological journal. On average, articles in this journal are cited forty times in four years. The article in question was cited only six times. This resulted in a low score for the article. The error here was that a macro-picture (the average score of articles in the journal) was applied to the micro-level (the concrete article about dolphins), leading to the conclusion that this was a poor performance. However, only six articles about the swimming behaviour of dolphins appeared in the four years concerned. The above article was cited in all of these articles, which was an excellent performance.[12]

This mechanism goes hand in hand with another mechanism: the greater the distance between the external actor using output figures and the professional producing output figures, the more the external actor will perceive the figures as unambiguous. The professional producing an output figure is close to the primary process and knows the reality behind the figure. The output figure is one of the sources of information that acquires a meaning in combination with other (in many cases qualitative) sources of information. The professional knows, for example, that many muskrats have been caught but that this is explained by not catching rats in winter. The output figure is far more important as a source of information for an external actor who is far removed from this primary process. If these figures are indeed regarded as reliable figures, the external actor in question will feel justified in carrying out interventions based on them. Anyone who asks for the reality behind the figures or for the assumptions and aggregation rules used will soon draw suspicion to himself that he does not want to face the facts.

Research by Bowerman and Hawksworth into performance measurement among local authorities demonstrates this mechanism. They conclude that external reviewers collect the information about the performance of local authorities and that it is often dealt with in a rigid manner. Directives based on comparisons between authorities are issued about performance or about savings that may be achieved in individual municipalities. This rigid attitude ignores that 'what is true in general may not be true universally and without qualification because circumstances alter cases'. Once it is clear that performance measurement is used in this way, the result is predictable: performance measurement is a form of nuisance to local authorities; they should try to prevent it as far as possible.[13]

A measured performance can thus have two meanings: the meaning given by professionals and the meaning given by external actors. If these meanings diverge, strategic behaviour might emerge. The professional who knows that the ambiguous figures will be interpreted as being unambiguous may try to influence them by game-playing in order to prevent wrong interpretations.

6 Performance measurement drives out the professional attitude: no quality, no system responsibility, more bureaucracy

Professional products and services are always a trade-off between a number of values.[14] A museum that builds up a collection works from a variety of values: its collection should have cultural value, should preserve heritage, serves an educational purpose, should make (future) scientific research possible and should serve the public. The essence of the museum profession is the constant trade-off made between these values. The values may conflict: a new piece in a collection may serve the collection's cultural value, but might not attract many visitors.

Performance indicators measure quantities and will therefore mainly be applied to measurable and clearly definable interests; for museums these are the numbers of visitors. As regards the other interests (e.g. scientific research), the performance indicators are always a derivative (e.g. the number of documents consulted by researchers). The result is predictable: when only visitor numbers are relevant, the integrity or cultural value of the collection may suffer.[15] Performance measurement may drive out the professional attitude because the museum concentrates too much on the well-defined tasks.[16]

- I refer here to a remarkable study by Iaquinto, which is illustrative even though it concerns the private sector. Iaquinto examined the influence of winning the Deming Prize for 'total quality management' (TQM) by Japanese companies on their performance. He found that, for the vast majority of them, the winning of the award is followed by a drop in performance. For TQM, a large number of performance indicators exist, which are always a derivative, since it concerns the 'contested' concept of quality. Companies take three years to maximize their performance on these indicators. Consequently, they will focus strongly on these indicators for a longer time and neglect other aspects of their business operations. The result is that their performance will decline. Focusing on performance indicators drives out the professional attitude of seeking constant trade-offs between different interests.[17]

- An important characteristic of professionals is that they have a high tolerance of ambiguity. The profession they practise is complex, and in some cases the same situation allows for several and mutually conflicting interpretations. For example, a rat catcher's task is to catch as many rats as possible. All the same, he has to let a number of rats go, even though he is able to catch them. If he caught too many rats, the remaining ones would have so much physical space that they would produce very strong and fertile offspring. This risk will be far less if sufficient numbers of rats are left to survive. Tolerance of ambiguity is an important characteristic of other professionals, such as judges and surgeons. A court has to deliver judgements. In some cases it may be wise to deliver no judgement at all, because a case may also be dealt with informally, which might be more effective. A hospital has to prevent waiting lists. In some cases, however, waiting lists are functional; for example, because they allow patients time for reflection, after which they might abandon the idea of an operation. The rat catcher who does not catch rats, the court that does not deliver judgements and the hospital that allows waiting lists to grow: each may demonstrate professionalism. In some cases a rat catcher should not catch rats, a court should not deliver judgements and a hospital should not clear a waiting list. Systems of performance measurement cannot handle this ambiguity: catching rats, delivering judgements and clearing waiting lists are rewarded. These systems may therefore harm the essence of a profession.

This driving-out mechanism might occur within, but also between organizations. Particularly in the public sector, organizations have a *system responsibility*. Organizations should make the professional insights they develop available to other organizations in the public sector. Performance measurement may force out this system responsibility.

- Research by Fiske and Ladd showed that schools which compete with each other in terms of performance are less prepared to share their 'best practices' (regarding methods of education, how to deal with differences between pupils, health, and so on) with each other. Performance measurement has a negative influence on the relations which schools maintain with each other.[18]
- The underlying mechanism here is that performance measurement forces an organization to optimize its own performance. This makes performance measurement a disincentive for cooperation. It may consequently lead to intra-organizational or inter-organizational compartmentalization (units optimize their own performance and cooperate insufficiently).

> • Research also shows that organizations scoring well in a system of perform-
> ance measurement have invested heavily in procedural and organizational
> amenities, thus enabling them to meet the requirements of the system of per-
> formance measurement.[19] There is a unit, for example, that registers each
> product of an organization and sees to it that the individual members of the
> organization provide it with all the information.

Now there is no objection to this at all, although the research mentioned
also shows that, on paper, these organizations perform better than organizations with fewer such amenities, but do not do so in reality.

The explanation is easy to guess: a unit whose main task is to register
and account for an organization's performance is likely to be competent
to do it so as to allow its own organization to score as high as possible
in the system.

> Research by Power points in that direction. Organizations in the United Kingdom
> prove to be adept at massaging reality in such a way that it becomes accessible
> to the controller. Making information 'auditable' has a higher priority than actu-
> ally solving problems.[20] One beneficial effect of performance measurement is that
> it may reinforce an organization's external orientation (see Chapter 1). It may now
> be stated that the picture may also be the reverse: performance measurement
> may also reinforce an organization's internal orientation.

7 Performance measurement leads to copying, not learning

One advantage of performance measurement is that it may bring about
learning processes. The availability of output figures allows comparison
between organizations: court A has shorter lead times than court B, university A needs fewer support staff than university B. Once differences
have been identified, court B and university B can start looking for the best
practices of court A and university A, and can thus learn.

Ideally, benchmarking means that an organization is inspired by the experiences of others, but subsequently makes its own choices. However, benchmarking may degenerate into silly copying: the best practices are simply
transplanted from organization A to organization B. Copying is always
risky, because it is never clear *what* exactly is the *best practice* that has to
be imitated and whether an organization will *accept or reject* the transplant.

Suppose organization A is concerned about the volume of support staff: the HR and Finance departments seem large and the staff–line ratio appears high. By means of a benchmark, the organization analyses what staff–line ratio other, similar organizations have. One of these organizations, organization B, is found to have a low ratio. This organization is then asked to explain this ratio. Organization B is found to have a highly decentralised staff organization. This best practice is then transplanted to organization B. This process includes a number of major obstacles:

- *Reduction of complexity.* The first question is what the reality is behind B's low ratio. How are staff and line employees counted? What is the definition of a staff employee and what of a line employee? What tasks are allocated to the staff and what to the line? What kind of support do the line employees need? Does the organization have a culture in which a line employee is given maximal support or one in which a line employee is as self-supporting as possible? Numerous other questions may be asked, which make one thing clear: the ratio is a figure behind which there is a far more complex reality. The figure *reduces* this complexity.
- *Rationalization of success.* The second question is whether the explanation for the low ratio is correct. Is it actually the decentralized organization that explains this ratio, or are there other explanations? There are always additional or even alternative explanations: the high level of the staff employees, the physical location of the staff employees, the organization of the primary processes, the rotation of the staff employees around the various organization units and so on. The decentralized organization may even be a disaster for service provision, but the line employees may have kept the service provision running through all kinds of makeshift measures. Decentralization may be just a very small part of the explanation for the ratio. Alternatively, organization B might have an even lower ratio if the staff units were centrally organized. The explanation for the figure is therefore always a *rationalization* of the reality, which is partly fictitious by definition.
- *Poor copy of reality.* The third question is whether organization A is actually able to copy the best practice. What actually is the best practice? Is it decentralization? And what in particular? Or is it decentralization + a high level of staff employees? Or is it decentralization + a high level of staff employees + a particular organization of the primary processes? In many cases, the best practice copied by organization A is a poor copy of the reality in organization B.
- *Success is not always transplantable.* The fourth question is whether the best practice of organization B actually fits the structure and

culture of organization A. In medical terms: will organization A accept the transplant of the best practice of B or reject it?

The above problems will arise when benchmarking degenerates into unthinkingly copying best practices elsewhere. In such a case, copying best practices can hardly work out. Comparing benchmarking to karaoke: a poor copy of reality, Ridderstrale and Nordstrom argue that 'benchmarking never gets you to the top'.[21]

8 Performance measurement leads to punishment of performance

Performance measurement rewards productivity, but its effect may also be that productivity is punished. There are four mechanisms that account for this effect.

Everybody performs better and therefore receives a financial sanction

First, if performance measurement is linked to financial reward, there is an incentive for the organizations concerned to increase productivity. This increase in productivity does not lead to reward, however, if the budget to be divided among these organizations remains the same. This is a well-known problem: there is a previously fixed price per product, and the organizations concerned increase their total output to such a level that the budgets allocated to the organizations exceed the total budget available. The result may be that management must cut prices per product later, once output has been established. This may create the impression that better performance is not rewarded.

A transparent and well-performing organization is vulnerable

Performance measurement leads to transparency and may be an incentive for production. This may cause a rise in output on a given budget and, the reasoning will go, the same performance can probably be achieved on a lower budget. Bordewijk and Klaassen point to the phenomenon that an organization which invests in efficiency is taking a risk: management may translate this into a lower budget for the following year, performance remaining equal. An affiliate organization not investing in efficiency is rewarded with a budget that remains the same, performance remaining equal.[22]

The mechanism here is that, thanks to transparency and good performance, higher targets may be imposed, whereas an organization that is unable to offer this transparency (in the worst case because it performs badly) is 'rewarded' with equal targets and resources. In time, this creates the impression that good performance is punished and poor performance is rewarded. If this impression becomes embedded, it warrants various other forms of perverting behaviour.

An organization performs better in a non-performing environment and therefore receives a financial sanction (1)

Suppose a professional organization shows a rise in productivity while other organizations lag seriously behind. This causes the well-performing organization to grow and the non-performing ones to fall behind (entirely in line with the aims of performance measurement). At some stage, the non-performing part of the organization approaches a critical lower limit. The ultimate consequence of performance measurement would be that the 'non-performer' disappears, but in many situations that is impossible.

This is because such a consequence presupposes that the manager has a sufficient degree of freedom to take such a measure. Frequently, this is not the case: such a drastic consequence is subject to all sorts of (legal) constraints. This has an important implication: the cost of punishing non-performance is likely to be higher than the benefit of rewarding performance.

It should be added that the cause and effect of non-performance may be debatable. What is the explanation for the situation in which the non-performing organization has ended up? Two opposite lines of reasoning are imaginable:

- The organization fails to perform. The system of performance measurement makes this visible and draws its conclusions. The cause of the situation in which the organization finds itself is therefore its poor performance.
- The organization fails to perform. The cause of this is the system of performance measurement. When performance is below standard, the system applies a financial sanction. This means that the resources of the relevant organization part will diminish, causing performance to fall even further, causing another financial sanction and so on. Performance measurement means that the rich get richer and the poor get poorer.

The management of an organization therefore has to make a trade-off, the outcome of which is predictable:

* The cost of punishing non-performance is higher than that of rewarding good performance.
* There is a line of reasoning available which concludes that the system of performance measurement is the cause of the poor performance.

The result of this reasoning is that the non-performing organization part is offered help, in some cases at the expense of the well-performing organization part. This reasoning may be correct, but it may also be an occasional argument. If the latter is the case, there is a performance paradox: any party performing well in a non-performing environment will eventually be punished.

An organization performs better in a non-performing environment and therefore receives a financial sanction (2)

A variant of this mechanism occurs in organizations providing substitutable products and services. If this is the case, there is a strong incentive for performance in such organizations. After all, in the event of non-performance the manager has an alternative: he can substitute the products and services of organization A for those of organization B.

An organization providing non-substitutable products and services has a weaker incentive for performance because it is a monopolist. It is not attractive for the manager to punish non-performance of such an organization, since this will cause problems: the product or the service can no longer be provided. This gives rise to an incentive structure as summarized in Table 2.1.

In a mixed environment – both substitutable and non-substitutable products and services – the incentive structure also suggests that performance

Table 2.1 Performance measurement involving substitutable and non-substitutable products

	Performance measurement from the perspective of the organization	Performance measurement from the perspective of management
Product/service substitutable	Incentive to perform	Incentive to sanction
Product/service not substitutable	No incentive to perform	No incentive to sanction

is not rewarded. One organization has strong incentives for performance and is punished if it fails to perform; the other organization will suffer hardly any consequences of non-performance.

The last two mechanisms make clear that performance measurement does not work when sharp differences exist between organizations. This is a paradoxical conclusion: performance measurement stimulates performance, but only if the levels of performance by the organizations do not differ too much. In many cases, this causes performance measurement to be designed in such a way that it cannot cause excessive differences between organizations. This can be achieved by all sorts of moderating mechanisms or by defining performance indicators so as to take expected differences in performance into account beforehand.

9 Explanations

What is the explanation for the above picture? Why do systems of performance measurement create the above perverse effects?

Performance measurement is poor and unfair

The most important characteristic of a professional organization is that the primary process is complex and knowledge-intensive. This has a number of consequences for the organization shaping this process.

- The primary process requires special *expertise*, which is difficult to standardize. This renders an organization always highly dependent on the expertise of the organization's members. Much of the expertise is 'tacit knowledge': it is difficult to specify and to formalize.
- Earlier I mentioned the need to make trade-offs. Professional activities like those of a museum manager are *multiple-value* activities: they must meet several conflicting values. Such a trade-off should always meet the standard of 'locality': it should match the special circumstances of a concrete case and may therefore differ from one situation to another. This is why a fixed standard for the trade-off is not available in most cases.
- A public service professional provides services by *interacting* with the environment (citizens, companies, other authorities, fellow professionals). Organizing this interaction and using it to improve the quality of the services rendered is part of this professionalism.
- A professional is adaptive and will learn. New developments are linked to his or her existing expertise, which creates new expertise. Expertise develops in processes of interaction between a professional and his or

her environment. This makes professional development an ongoing *process*.

- Finally, professional expertise and skills are difficult to transfer. In many cases, a professional will learn only by interacting with third parties (since his or her expertise is 'tacit' and frequently does not become explicit until he or she interacts with third parties). Professionalism is also difficult to teach, isolated as it is from the concrete performance of a professional activity. Every form of formalization of the profession (in handbooks, manuals, but also in formal systems of accountability) fails to do sufficient justice to the richness of the profession.

Each of these characteristics is inconsistent with a system of performance measurement. I shall work this out using an example from the police organization.

Three armed raids have occurred in a shopping centre over a four-month period. This has caused unrest and the question is what action the police should take in the area concerned. The answer depends on, for example:

- the geography of the neighbourhood;
- the shopping patterns;
- the extent to which the shopkeepers are organized;
- the urgency of other problems facing the area team;
- the architectural design of the shopping centre.

A police official's first opinion about the most effective strategy will be based on these and many other considerations. It results partly from objectivizable facts and circumstances, partly from the professional's 'tacit knowledge': his or her experience of this type of crime in this neighbourhood. When various police officials, each with their own 'tacit knowledge', exchange their experiences and knowledge, a rich image of an effective strategy may emerge. The choice of the eventual strategy is made by interacting with the actors directly involved (the management of the shopping centre's car park, the shopkeepers' association, the shopping centre's security firm, and municipal departments). The result of these consultations is a number of agreements with these actors with the aim of bringing about a drop in the number of raids.

This strategy development is a learning process: the strategy is adjusted on the basis of the experiences of other professionals and the views of the actors concerned. This process of interaction continues once the agreements are implemented.

The idea underlying performance measurement is that the performance of professional organizations may be standardized in a set of performance indicators. This is inconsistent with the professional character of many organizations (see the description of the police organization). From the professional's perspective, the application of performance measurement to professional processes leads to poor information.

- The police organization's strategy comprises a large number of actions. However, this rich image is only partly reflected in the performance measurement. This may lead to the judgement that no justice is done to the professional's expertise. A system of performance measurement will never produce a rich image of professional activities.
- An adequate appraisal of the strategy of the police organization should also reckon with the 'throughput': the efforts made by the organization to arrive at an effective strategy with the parties concerned. In output thinking, this is just expenditure to arrive at the product; in professional thinking, they are crucial to the appraisal of the approach of the police.
- When services are rendered by interacting with the actors concerned, the eventual performance also depends on the effort of the other actors. As a rule, systems of performance measurement do not recognize this.

Suppose professionals find a system of performance measurement to be a poor system: it is not suitable for arriving at a rich judgement of performance. Suppose the management nevertheless uses it. Many professionals will then feel justified in using the possibilities offered by the system opportunistically. To summarize: those who use a poor system of performance measurement treat professionals unfairly and invite perverting behaviour. Once such a course of action has developed, it may become institutionalized in the course of time: opportunistic use is completely normal and is therefore no longer regarded as opportunism.

Performance measurement is not dynamic

A second justification for opportunistic use is that a system of performance measurement tends to be static. At a particular moment in time it considers the products supplied at that moment. This does insufficient justice to the dynamic of professional activities.

- New performance does not always match the existing system of performance measurement. New products may develop which are not visible in the performance measurement, with existing output falling sharply. This may suggest that the performance of the professional in question is declining, but the conclusion is that performance measurement is not dynamic.

- It is equally important that this dynamism does not involve the products of the organization, but the *processes* that precede it. A university produces a certain output: for example, Master's degrees. This output is the result of a process, in which all sorts of things happen due to developments in the university's environment (e.g. a new type of student enters who is different from earlier types; there are new technological developments). The professional is active in this process and deals with questions that are only partly reflected in output targets. What subjects does the university offer? How intense is the guidance given to students? What additional activities are organized for and with the students? Does the university have an international exchange programme? Does the education involve the use of information and communications technology? How does the university deal with changes in the learning styles of new generations of students? These questions concern the essence of the profession and result in considerable dynamics in professional organizations.

The more complex a product (e.g. it is generated in a network of dependencies; it is multiple: see Table 1.1), the greater the dynamics because more actors are involved and because more values must be weighed. The problem here is that many systems of performance measurement are necessarily static because of the functions for which they are used. When budgets are allocated or a 'benchmark' is made with the help of performance measurement, the system requires a certain stability. Only then is comparison over a certain time possible and the system is able to fulfil its function.

From a professional perspective, dynamics of performance measurement are therefore desirable, while from a management and control perspective the accent is on stability. The risk of this is that performance measurement will degenerate into an accounting activity and will lack dynamism.

10 Question: How to value the ambiguous image of performance measurement?

The criticism of performance measurement in this chapter is that a professional will perceive it as poor, unfair and not dynamic. This justifies perverting behaviour: the system is fed with information that serves only to show up the position of the professional to the best advantage (strategic behaviour, using the veiling effect of figures, no innovation, optimizing input, minimizing throughput, accepting no system responsibility, sacrificing quality).

An ambiguous picture of performance measurement has now been outlined: it may be beneficial, but it may also cause perverse effects. This raises the question as to how these images relate to each other.

I give a first answer in Chapter 3: an important risk is that the perverse effect of performance measurement may eventually drive out the beneficial effect. In the following chapters I go on to discuss the question of how the conflict between beneficial and perverse effects may be turned to good use.

Chapter 3

The dynamics of performance measurement:

Five laws

1 Introduction

An interesting question is how the behaviour of performance measurement systems changes in the course of time. Do the positive or the perverse effects dominate? Do systems retain their elegance or do they become bloated? Performance measurement systems provide the manager with a quantified and limited perspective on the profession. Is any attention given to other, difficult-to-quantify aspects of professional performance? Or does the perspective tend to narrow and to limit itself to the quantified performance? What about the attention professionals and managers pay to performance measurement? Does habituation set in as time goes by, with waning attention for performance measurement? Or do they continue to be alert to these systems and do these systems retain their positive incentives?

All these questions relate to the dynamics of performance measurement systems. They are discussed in this chapter by defining five laws.

2 The Law of Decreasing Effectiveness

Chapter 2 lists the positive and perverse effects of performance measurement. Under what conditions will the positive, or conversely the perverse, effects dominate?

The answer to this question depends strongly on what *function* the production figures have. Typically, production figures may have a low or a high impact. Their impact is low if their function is limited to transparency (see also Chapter 1 on the functions of performance measurement). Figures are published, but otherwise have no direct consequences for the professional. Their impact is high if they have immediate and severe consequences, as in the following examples:

- *Financial sanctions*. A positive or negative financial sanction is linked to the production figure. For example, the future budget may be dependent on performance. An underperforming organization receives a punishment, whereas one that overperforms is rewarded with a bonus. The impact is high because future budgets largely determine an organization's opportunities.

- *Naming and shaming.* An organization's production figures may be published alongside those of other organizations in the form of a ranking, declaring publicly which organizations perform best and which worst. The impact is high because a low ranking may influence the choices made by customers, not to mention future personnel, who would prefer to work for an organization with a high ranking.

- *Administrative and managerial interventions.* Production figures that differ from an average – whether in time or across organizations – are more likely to attract the attention of politicians and managers than those close to an average. In particular, organizations that emerge under an average run the risk of administrative or managerial intervention, which means more interference with the daily course of events, a change of structure, tighter supervision and so on. This is an unattractive proposition, because it erodes an organization's degrees of freedom. However, an above-average score can also be unattractive, because, for example, it can lead to new, even higher production targets.

There are two respects in which a low-impact performance measurement may be appreciated. The first is that it probably has few incentives for improving an organization's performance. From the professional's perspective, the system is innocuous: the production figures have hardly any function.

The second is that a low impact is sufficient for effective performance measurement. Suppose a professional organization is able to exhibit only mediocre production figures. Professionals who observe this state of affairs may feel that it is a matter of professional honour to improve the organization's performance. By appealing to professional honour, the figures have a self-healing effect.

If this self-healing mechanism does not manifest itself, an argument for contrary treatment is attractive: if a low impact yields no performance incentives, it is desirable to increase the impact. The idea, at least, is that as the potential impact increases, the positive effects of performance measurement (see Chapter 1) will increase accordingly.

However, the potential impact of performance measurement can be so high that it constitutes an incentive for perverse behaviour. If an organization's budget depends heavily on production, there will be strong reasons to behave strategically, to ignore professional values, to neglect innovation

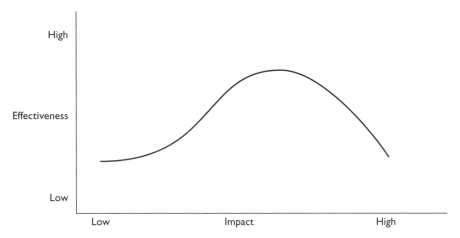

Figure 3.1 The Law of Decreasing Effectiveness

and so on. When an organization's performance is quantified and then published in the form of a ranking, incentives for perverse conduct are also created. The impact of a low ranking can be enormous, and organizations will therefore endeavour to limit it. This is the Law of Decreasing Effectiveness: if performance measurement has a high impact, the effectiveness of performance measurement declines, because strong incentives for perverse behaviour arise (see Figure 3.1).

Test results at schools

This law is illustrated by an investigation into output financing in the Amsterdam education system.[1]

At some time in the past, dissatisfaction arose in Amsterdam with the performance of primary schools, which was far below the national average.[2] The municipal administration introduced quantified performance agreements in order to deal with this issue. Agreements were made with the schools to bring the level of Amsterdam schoolchildren, as measured in the National Institute for Educational Measurement tests, up to the national average. Targets were agreed for each school, in line with the school's pupil population. Schools that failed to achieve the agreed results would be called to account, and could suffer cuts in their funding.[3] 'Naming and shaming' was also an important component of this policy, because the aldermen concerned were very active in communicating their policy to the media.

Thus this was a situation in which performance measurement had a high impact.

The introduction of this system had several consequences:[4]

- The average Amsterdam test results were rising, and in a number of respects were even better than elsewhere in the country. The gap between the poorest performing schools and the average also narrowed significantly.
- Automated practice programmes for certain parts of the test were used more heavily than before. The opinions on this trend are mixed: while practice is good for scores, it also leads to a narrowing of education.
- The main point measured by the test is basic skills. The increased interest in test scores meant that schools were paying more attention than before to these basic skills. Again the opinions are mixed. Some schools considered this development to be both correct and desirable, believing that the curriculum had paid too little attention to basic skills in the past. Other schools considered the additional attention to basic skills to be less desirable educationally, but that it had been prompted by the need for high scores in the test. They perceived the focus on basic skills as a form of strategic behaviour.
- Weak pupils appeared either to have avoided taking the test, or their test data were not reported.
- Invigilators used certain signals to warn schoolchildren of mistakes they might be making while taking the test.

Visser concludes from this list that the Amsterdam policy was ineffective. Although the scores were higher, they were a result in part of strategic behaviour (e.g. reporting sick, invigilator behaviour) and in part of behaviour that in some, though not all, cases may be described as strategic (e.g. too much attention to basic skills, too much attention to practice tests). Furthermore, as test results degenerate into an external instrument for reporting to the alderman – who is demanding a higher average – the test's reliability and internal usefulness as a good-quality assessment of schoolchildren is declining.[5]

The Law of Decreasing Effectiveness leads to a paradox: the greater a manager's efforts to manage on performance measurement, the stronger the incentive for professionals to exhibit perverse behaviour. More control leads to more negative effects.

I repeat that professionals often feel justified in bringing about perverse effects. The nature of many products of public and professional organizations make them ineligible for quantified performance measurement (see Chapter 1 on Type 2 products). If performance measurement is applied for products of this kind regardless, and moreover has a high impact, the situation may be viewed by the professional as extremely unfair. A hospital with leading surgeons who draw patients that have been written off as untreatable elsewhere will inevitably have a high mortality rate. The hospital concerned would then come extremely low in any ranking based on mortality rates that might subsequently be compiled and published. This 'naming and shaming' is so unfair that it may legitimate perverse behaviour. Someone who is treated unfairly will feel justified in perverting the system.

3 Interlude: performance measurement in the American corporate culture

The literature contains many warnings against a hierarchical use of performance measurement.[6] It is apparently tempting to use performance measurement in a hierarchical way.[7]

If achieving performance has a high impact, it can manifest itself in a hierarchical management style. The manager obliges the professionals to achieve a quantified performance, and if they fail to do so, drastic sanctions will follow. A clear illustration of just how ill-advised a hierarchical use of performance measurement of this kind can be is given in a study by Philippe d'Iribarne on the use of performance measurement in the American corporate culture.[8] Performance measurement has deep roots in the United States, not, however, in a vertical, hierarchical management style but in a horizontal, contractual one. D'Iribarne says that this is essential for the success of performance measurement:

- The actors involved realize that objectives and assessment criteria are no more than a rough guide to the performance actually delivered. This actual performance is always more complex than can be captured in the formal objectives and performance indicators. As a result, there is no relationship between the formal performance and the employee's remuneration for a majority of the objectives realized.
- The performance mentality is embedded in the value of 'fairness'. The actors involved deal with each other fairly, which means, for example, that the fact that a delivered performance is only an estimate of reality is open for discussion, which discourages opportunistic or perverse behaviour.
- Another contractual value is reasonableness. One of the implications of this value is that actors are willing to change objectives and

performance indicators if it is reasonable to do so. Indeed, change is always negotiable in a contractual relationship, which cannot be taken for granted in a hierarchical relationship because it erodes the functions of performance measurement.

- The literature on performance measurement occasionally points to the risk of a tendency to rely on feelings of fear: anyone failing to satisfy a certain performance will be punished.[9] D'Iribarne points out that the performance contract in American culture also *binds the manager*. The manager too has obligations and is expected to fulfil them.

- Performance management mentality is coupled with sanctions that may be imposed if some agreed performance is not realized. However, the imposition of sanctions for non-fulfilment is subject to procedures intended to *protect the subordinate against arbitrariness* on this point.

- Finally, it is noteworthy that the parties are aware that performance agreements have *two functions*: a 'managerial' function[10] and a political function. The political function involves parties accepting the necessity of making the performance that an organization delivers clear to the outside world, and the possibility of conflict between the two functions. The manager therefore sometimes tolerates non-fulfilment of agreements, whereas the subordinate tolerates the fact that the performance on paper may be a distortion – to his disadvantage – of the actual performance.

Superiors and subordinates therefore enter into performance agreements that are embedded in values such as honesty, fairness and reasonableness. These values are a disincentive for the kind of perverse behaviour described in Chapter 2.

4 The Law of Mushrooming

The strength of performance measurement is that it is a simple means of giving account. An organization's performance may be summed up in a limited number of product definitions, indicators and production figures. However, performance measurement systems can also become bloated, and lose their simplicity in the process. This phenomenon may be described as the Law of Mushrooming. Mushrooming can manifest itself in numerous ways:

- the refinement of existing product definitions and indicators;
- the need for lengthy explanations for product definitions and indicators;

- the creation of new product definitions and indicators;
- the introduction of rules for measuring or estimating production;
- the appearance of new rules for dealing with exceptions.[11]

There are several explanations for this law. First, professionals learn to exploit the freedom the system offers them for strategic behaviour. The natural managerial response to this strategic behaviour is refinement: for example, by tightening product definitions, to prevent professionals putting forward performance that exists only on paper, with no connection to the real world. Management suspicions may be aroused if an organization produces outstanding output results year after year. Perhaps the input is being optimized. One of the possible responses is obvious: new indicators must be developed for the input, which enables input–output analysis.

The second explanation is that performance measurement systems focus on only a few aspects of professional performance. A possible consequence is that the professional feels unfairly treated, because, for example, the professional scores poorly in the performance measurement system, even though the actual performance is considerably better. A professional who is confronted with a situation of this kind has a strong incentive to inflate the system. For example, he or she will argue that he or she wants new indicators added to the system in order to create a more realistic view of his or her performance.

A third explanation is that both the professional and managerial levels are always dynamic. On the professional level, a university that is confronted with an increasing number of students of foreign origin will be keen to see this new reality reflected in the production figures. On the administrative level, when introducing a new policy, new product definitions and production figures may be needed. New indicators may also be called for if an issue attracts new political attention.

The central explanation of the mushrooming phenomenon is easy to distil from the above explanations: performance measurement provides only a limited view of reality, which can create problems for both the manager and the professional. The natural response is to extend the performance measurement, thus adding new product definitions and indicators to the system. However, doing so weakens these systems: they lose their elegance. In the course of time they become so complex that they lose their positive impact.

A simple example may clarify how easily this Law of Mushrooming starts to operate. Many universities have introduced output control systems, which means that research groups are judged on numbers of publications. A distinction may be made between types of publications, for example between articles in scientific journals, books and professional publications. The production may be rewarded, for example, by attaching financial rewards to each type of publication. It is also conceivable to award points for each type of publication and to insist that each researcher earns some minimum number of points in a year.

Suppose one of the types of publications is an 'international scientific book', to which a financial reward, or a number of points, is attached. As the rewards or the number of points per publication increase, the incentives for strategic behaviour will likewise increase. It is not hard to imagine how the mushrooming process starts.

A *manager* who wishes to curtail strategic behaviour is soon confronted with the following questions:

- Should the book be of a minimum size?
- Are only English language books considered to be international, or do Spanish and Mandarin books count too? What about French and German books?
- Does a second edition count as a separate international scientific book, and if not, does a second, entirely revised edition, count?
- How should one deal with books that are a compilation of previously published articles?
- How is the scientific nature of the book to be determined? By requiring that the publisher works with a system of referees? Or by insisting that a book is brought out by a scientific publisher? How, then, does one define 'scientific publisher'? Is a book written for teaching purposes also scientific?
- How many international books are there if a book is first published in English and later in Spanish and Mandarin: one, two or three?
- Whose books actually attract a reward? Also retired academics? Guest researchers?

A *professional* confronted with this system would be bound to find unfair elements that need to be rectified.

- Suppose only books in the major languages (i.e. English, Spanish and Mandarin) were accepted as 'international'. Should exceptions be made for disciplines where tradition dictates a different language; for example, for theologians, who frequently publish in German, or for lawyers, whose object of study is the national laws and regulations?
- Suppose the number of books per researcher in some disciplines is far higher than in others; for example, because the disciplines concerned involve subjects that are commercially attractive to publishers.

Should exceptions then be made for the other disciplines, for example by giving them more money or points for each book?

Many other questions could be added to this list, but the example illustrates that a simple description of a product can spark off a mushrooming process.

It is interesting to identify the conditions under which the Law of Mushrooming operates. There are at least four situations in which this law is likely to apply:

- *When the distance between the assessor and the assessed is wide.* The greater the distance, the less information the assessor has on the context of the performance. A very remote assessor will find it hard to judge whether a book constitutes a major academic performance or a scientific trifle. If the assessor is closer to the object of the assessment (for example, because he is familiar with the field), his task will be simpler.
- *In an atmosphere of considerable mistrust.* The greater the mistrust between the assessor and the assessed, the stronger the incentives on both to inflate the system. The assessor will be wary of strategic behaviour and wish to make the system watertight, whereas the party being assessed will be apprehensive of an unfair opinion, and will have incentives for perverse behaviour.
- *A system's age.* As a system becomes older, both the assessor and the assessed will become more adept at coping with it. Both will be more aware of the system's weaknesses, which again may give both of them incentives to eliminate or exploit them.
- *A high impact of the consequences.* A fourth explanation again involves the Law of Decreasing Effectiveness. The higher the impact of a production figure, the stronger the incentive for mushrooming.

Mushrooming is a dangerous phenomenon which may erode the essence of a performance measurement. The essence is that it is an elegant means of accounting. Although it may not do proper justice to the complexity of professional performance, every system demands a trade-off between simplicity and complexity.[12] A system that becomes ever more bloated loses its simplicity and, as mentioned above, ultimately also its controlling effect.

An important paradox also surrounds mushrooming. On the one hand: however bloated, specific and refined a performance measurement system becomes, there is almost invariably some scope for new forms of strategic behaviour. This is an undesirable situation. However, the hypothetical case of a watertight system would be equally undesirable. A watertight system, which therefore offers no scope at all for strategic behaviour, is almost always unfair for Type 2 products (see Chapter 1). It may seriously erode a system's legitimacy and possibly lead to strategic behaviour elsewhere. Incentives for strategic behaviour always remain, and as long as they exist, so does the risk of mushrooming.

5 The Law of Collective Blindness

Production figures always give a distorted picture of reality. Anyone trusting in the figures alone is blind to the reality behind them. Smith once referred to this phenomenon as myopia: a form of short-sightedness caused by putting too much faith in the production figure.[13] For many perverse effects, this short-sightedness manifests itself mainly on a managerial level. The professional will often be able to see that good production figures are being put forward at the expense of innovation, as a result of strategic behaviour, or as a result of input optimization. The manager, who has less knowledge of the professional processes, will be more likely to suffer from myopia. However, short-sightedness may also appear on the professional level:

- New staff, who are unfamiliar with the prevailing professional values, may gain the impression that achieving the production figure is a professional value.
- An important characteristic of the professional is a high tolerance of complexity, more so than the manager. A researcher will know, for example, that he or she has to perform both application-oriented and fundamental research. A performance measurement system as described above may create strong incentives for ignoring application-oriented research. The only research to be performed will be that which leads to publications in scientific journals. The tolerance for complexity therefore declines.
- The professional also has a high tolerance of ambiguity. An example would be the hospital mentioned in Chapter 2, which aims to cut waiting lists, but is also aware that waiting lists can have a positive function. This ambiguity can also disappear under the influence of performance measurement. The hospital will do everything in its power to reduce waiting lists, even if doing so leads to more inefficiencies and other disadvantages.

The obvious risk attached to collective blindness is that a performance will be delivered which satisfies both the professional and the manager, although the performance concerned is at odds with what is happening in the real world, or with what is desirable professionally.

> An example would be the rat catcher who waits until the father and mother have produced a litter before catching and delivering the rats. Alternatively, he might lose his tolerance for ambiguity and catch rats, with no regard to whether enough rats are left to invade each other's territory and thus prevent explosive new population growth (Chapter 2). Either way, the rat catcher concerned may well attain a high production score. The *managerial layer* will be satisfied because the production trend is upward. The *rat catcher* will be satisfied because high production means a higher bonus, or because he will have warded off managerial interference. It is very likely that *planning and control staff* will also be satisfied, because the system they manage is being used. This is how collective blindness comes about in a situation of this kind: everyone is satisfied with the performance on paper, but the performance is being manipulated in the real world (the rats are not being caught but being bred) and is professionally undesirable (too few rats are being spared).

The above example may be harmless enough, but other examples of this law are significantly less so.

Shell's oil and gas reserves

The Anglo-Dutch oil company Shell suddenly announced in 2004 that its estimates of proven oil and gas reserves had been far too high.[14] The reserves that had been stated in the books had to be adjusted downwards by more than 20 per cent because they no longer complied with the criteria of the SEC, the United States stock market watchdog. The consequences for Shell were extremely serious: senior executives were forced to resign, and Shell was fined by the SEC and the FSA, the British stock market watchdog. The American judicial authorities started investigations into several Shell executives and ex-executives.

An important factor in the overestimate of the reserves was the performance management system operated by Shell. The bonuses of several important players in the organization were linked to the size of the proven reserves. The greater the reserves, the higher the bonuses. Shell's ex-head of exploration, Roel Murris, remarked, 'This encourages people to put too favourable a complexion on matters'.[15]

A 'proven reserve' is an ambiguous product, with no clear definition. The SEC says that a reserve is proven if a field could be 'economically and legally extracted or produced at the time of the reserve determination'.[16] This definition leaves considerable scope for interpretation, so that a 'proven reserve' is not open to objection. Furthermore, a 'proven reserve' is hard to quantify. Technologies exist for determining the size, but the uncertainty often remains higher than a factor of 2. Only when the fields are actually exploited does a clearer picture emerge.

The consequence for performance management is clear. Where ambiguous products are concerned, quantification of performance leaves considerable scope for strategic behaviour, which can be exploited by professionals when reporting the performance. As Roel Murris said, 'If you demand success from those who work for you, this is what you get. Especially if a financial or career bonus is attached.'[17]

The consequence is a peaceful equilibrium between managers and professionals. Management is satisfied with the impression that its objectives are being achieved. The professionals are satisfied by not having to put up with management interference, or even by being rewarded. The perverse information has taken root in the organization. There is a state of collective blindness.

The chances of this phenomenon occurring are particularly high when a performance management system does not change, with the same performance indicators remaining for years on end. In addition, if an organization has too few checks and balances (e.g. because its internal accountant is in a weak position), strong incentives exist for blocking any information that might disturb the peaceful equilibrium, or prompt discussion about the performance measurement system. Shell's external auditor Anton Barendrecht warned in three successive annual reports that the reliability of the estimates of the reserves was being strained by the link with bonuses. Dutch investigative journalists have received confirmation from multiple sources that the country managers within Shell put Anton Barendrecht in his place on several occasions. He was told to 'keep his hands off the bonuses'.[18] Meanwhile, many in the organization were under the impression that all was well with Shell.

6 The Law of Preservation of Perverted Systems

The picture of the dynamism of performance measurement that emerges when the three laws described above manifest themselves is sombre. Performance measurement is perverse, performance measurement systems become bloated, and may even lead to collective blindness. A possible consequence of all of the above is for performance measurement systems to be phased out. However, this measure is unnecessary. Perverse systems appear to be resistant to change. Once a system has taken root in an organization, it is not always a simple matter to abolish it or phase it out. There are two explanations for this phenomenon: systems may have a ritualizing tendency and systems have external owners, who have an interest in upholding the systems.

Ritualizing tendency

A moderate variant of the Law of Collective Blindness is that performance measurement has a tendency to ritualize. The first thing to happen is that the performance measurement loses its positive incentives. The perverse effects displace the positive effects. A production figure on paper says nothing about the reality behind it. The manager with an unshakeable confidence in performance measurement is the victim of the situation. He forms views on the delivered and desirable performance that have little connection with the real world. Management and profession become different and separate worlds. The professional world gives shape to the primary process. Professionals carry out their own activities in accordance with their own professional standards and values. They give shape to the primary process in line with their own insights, while they will have learned to feed the performance measurement system with the figures and information that management wants, so as to give the managerial level no cause to interfere.

Then there is the managerial world, which also has its own reality: planning and control cycles, annual reports, production schemes, production figures, long-term production planning schedules, analyses of the organization's past performance and so on.

Ritualization means that the professional level does not confront the managerial world and its paper reality, but rather upholds and even nourishes it. So long as the two worlds coexist and the professionals see enough opportunities to fend off hierarchical intervention, performance measurement is no threat to them. It is a ritual that ensures peaceful coexistence between management and professionals. This is a comfortable situation for the professionals: they have sufficient degrees of freedom to give shape to the primary process in accordance with their own insights. The ritual is also comfortable for the manager: he or she has the figures he or she wants, which usually confirm the desired trends. Thus the system nourishes the idea that everything is under control.

This may seem a fairly cynical picture, but the complaint that performance measurement is a ritual is often heard.[19] Research has shown that the same performance measurement system can have the confidence of managers and the distrust of professionals;[20] organizations invest heavily in performance measurement systems, which are then little used.[21]

Upholding this ritual is a form of behaviour that is partly unconscious and occurs quite naturally: from a professional perspective a system is dysfunctional, so professionals gradually learn how to cope with it, while the managerial level observes that the system is being used and is producing the desired information.

This picture of performance measurement as a ritual may be viewed positively, in that it prevents the professional from becoming ensnared in a performance measurement system that measures one or only a few aspects of professional reality. Performance measurement as a ritual may also be viewed negatively in that it obstructs the manager's view of the actual progress of the primary process and is therefore a breeding ground for poor management interventions. Whatever the case, it goes a long way towards explaining why neither managers nor professionals oppose perverted systems.

External owners of the systems

Once a system has been introduced, a network of stakeholders grows around it. The system not only plays a role in the relationship between manager and professional, but third parties also have interests in and consider themselves to be owners of it. This is visible on a grand scale in the United States in the form of the Government Performance and Results Act (GPRA). Broere called this a GPRA industry in Washington, consisting of the Office of Management and Budget, the American Court of Audit, the media, the staffs of representatives and senators, personnel of the major think tanks, consultants, and others.[22]

Among the important external owners are the following:

- Planning and control central departments, which administer the systems within the professional organization. They often have detailed knowledge of the systems, which provide them with much information. A familiar quip is that performance measurement systems can develop from 'tool to toy', in which they stop playing any meaningful role (i.e. a tool) between manager and professional and degenerate into a toy for the staff.
- Consultants, who are the external guards of performance measurement systems. They are frequently the developers of new tools and new applications, which invariably imply the promise of improved performance of the professional organization.
- The media, which are also very interested in performance measurement. Rankings of schools, hospitals and universities are news items. *The Times Higher Education Supplement* has published a ranking

of universities since 2004, with an important place given to the citations–faculty and students–faculty ratios. A ranking of this kind produced by external parties has specific characteristics. It is hard to modify the underlying measurement method. 'For consistency's sake, these rankings follow a similar pattern to last year's.'[23] While pointing out that universities are 'difficult to compare' and that there is 'no sign that a high-ranking university in our table is better than one more lowly ranked',[24] considerable significance is none the less attached to the ranking. 'Fascination with international comparisons is undiminished' and 'the search for the world's leading universities is surely unstoppable'.[25] Rankings can acquire a reputation. They appear annually, organizations look to see if they have gone up or down in the ranking, and the place in the ranking is seen as significant by third parties, including ministries, finance providers and other universities.

- Courts of audit. National and local courts of audit also often take refuge in a simple, objective–means mentality. Organizations have to formulate objectives, after which a judgement can be made on the degree to which they have been achieved. A professional organization that does not formulate keen objectives and demonstrates no clear and quantified performance may be performing well regardless. However, it is difficult for third parties to comment on the performance of systems of this kind. If objectives are formulated and quantified performance is made visible, judgements may be made on the performance.

This is not to say that the activities of these external owners are meaningless. The point is that these third parties have an interest in upholding systems of this kind, even if they have been perverted. Furthermore, these third parties are even more remote from the professional primary process than managers, and therefore have an even poorer view of the professional reality behind the figures.

7 The Law of Decreasing Political Attention

I finally discuss a fifth law. The question in Section 6 was why perverted systems are not phased out. There is also a second explanation. The *introduction* of performance measurement is often a sign of political resolve. The associated policy language often has a resolute undertone:

- 'professional freedom must not degenerate into informality';
- 'anyone who is given freedom and autonomy has the duty to be accountable';

- 'a person who performs must be rewarded';
- 'there is no longer any such thing as routine funding';
- 'anyone not performing should no longer be financed';
- 'the public has a right to know how professionals perform'.

When performance measurement systems are introduced, they take root in professional organizations. The laws described in this chapter may then manifest themselves: systems become perverted and bloated, and obstruct the view of the real world. However, *abolishing* performance measurement is a political dissatisfier: there is little honour to be gained in doing so. Furthermore, performance measurement has become institutionalized: it has external owners, it plays a role in the budget allocation, professionals learn through ritualization to live with it, and time and transformation costs are involved in introducing new allocation systems. A possible consequence is that political attention declines after performance measurement has been introduced, making it even more difficult to abolish systems of this kind.

8 Finally, an interesting question: Are the laws hard or soft?

The dynamics of performance measurement, with its five laws, raises an interesting question: Are the five laws inevitable? Are they hard laws? Or are they soft laws? Can performance measurement be structured so as to prevent these laws from operating? Is it conceivable for performance measurement to play a meaningful role in the relationship between management and professionals? And that the positive effect mentioned in Chapter 1 is not overshadowed by the perverse effects of Chapter 2? I address these topics in Part II, where I identify several rules of the game which are able to make performance measurement a meaningful activity.

Part II

Chapter 4

Design principles for performance measurement

I Introduction

Chapters 1 and 2 in Part I explained that performance measurement can have both positive and perverse effects; Chapter 3 went on to present five laws. The best case is when these laws do not operate. The worst case is when all five operate simultaneously, which means that the system is perverted (Law of Decreasing Effectiveness), is hugely bloated (Law of Mushrooming), is used anyway and leads to Collective Blindness, while insufficient incentives exist for abandoning the system (Law of the Preservation of Perverted Systems and Law of Decreasing Political Attention). If the five laws operate simultaneously, it means that a performance measurement system is perverted through and through, but is resistant at the same time: there are too few incentives to abandon it.

The question is how to prevent such a situation from arising. How can a performance measurement system be designed so that it provides little or no incentive for perverse behaviour?

The Law of Decreasing Effectiveness holds that the incentives concerned arise mainly if achieving production statistics has a considerable impact on the professionals or the professional organization. If the impact is high, professionals will often feel justified in perverting the system. If this observation is correct, the answer to the above question is obvious: systems will hardly be perverted, if at all, if they are *moderate* and are used in a *predictable* fashion. If the impact is limited and the use of performance measurement is predictable, the incentives for perverse behaviour decrease.

How can this moderate and predictable use be instrumentalized? It is possible by having the manager and professional agree a number of *rules of the game* for how to use a performance measurement system. These rules of the game have the same function as traffic regulations. Traffic regulations constrain the behaviour of vehicles and drivers and make interactions predictable. Rules of the game constrain the use of performance

Table 4.1 Three design principles for performance measurement

Value	Associated design principle
Trust, fairness	Interaction
Content	Variety
Liveliness	Dynamics

measurement and make the interaction between the manager and the professional predictable.

This chapter provides a brief introduction to the idea of rules of the game. I present three design principles for the rules of the game, which are then worked out as various concrete rules of the game in the following three chapters. Table 4.1 shows the three design principles.

I explained in Chapter 2 why professionals feel justified in perverting performance measurement. Because performance measurement is a poor way of forming a judgement, the professional feels unfairly treated. Furthermore, performance measurement is not a lively activity, but is simply a standardized way of rendering account.

- Performance measurement can be made less unfair by giving the professional the freedom to influence the definition of indicators, the measurement of performance and the assessment of performance. This approach translates into the design principle of interaction: trust is created if performance measurement results from an inter-action between the manager and the professional.
- Performance measurement is not so poor if more perspectives on the professional's performance are used than only a quantitative one. This idea translates into the design principle of variety: there must be freedom for multiple perspectives on the professional's performance.
- Performance measurement is less static if the manager concentrates not only on the products a professional delivers (e.g. the court judgement obtained), but also on the underlying processes (e.g. the conduct in the courtroom, the way in which the judgement was brought about).

The three design principles are briefly introduced below. Section 2 discusses the principle of interaction, Section 3 the principle of variety, and Section 4 the principle of dynamism.

2 Design principle 1: Interaction

An important value in performance measurement is trust. As soon as mistrust exists between management and the professional, there will be strong incentives to pervert the system. Trust of this kind is not automatic.

Trust will exist only if performance measurement is based on interaction between management and the professional, which means that the design of a performance measurement system results from interaction, while many moments of interaction are also involved in its use. This interaction is therefore concerned with decisions such as:

- How are products defined?
- What are the performance indicators for these products?
- How is performance measured and assessed?

Interaction means increasing the likelihood of support for the system, on the part of both the manager and the professional. It has a number of advantages.

- *Support for trade-offs of conflicting managerial and professional values*. The manager and the professional each represent legitimate values; for example, the need for accountability (management) and the importance of professionalism (professional). There may be a tension between these values. Interaction can create a form of performance measurement that does as much justice as possible to these values.
- *The manager and the professional are the owner of the system*. Furthermore, a system that is created through interaction has more owners and is therefore also significantly more likely to be used, as opposed to being merely an administrative accounting tool, for example.
- *Mutual trust*. Interaction can help build the trust held by management and the professional in their relationship with each other. A professional who knows that he can influence the way in which performance is measured and the way of dealing with measured performance will have more trust in the manager than if he views performance measurement as an intervention dropped from above. Because crucial steps in the performance measurement process result from interaction, performance measurement is also more predictable both for the manager and for the professional. Both may influence these steps, and both can trust that unilateral action will not occur.

3 Design principle 2: Variety

Public service is a multiple-value activity: there are multiple, partly contradictory, criteria involved, which demand ever-changing trade-offs. The multiplicity implies that an organization's products may be defined in many ways, and can therefore also be measured and assessed in many ways.

If so, judgement on professional production is always based on a certain variety of criteria. This variety may relate to product definitions, performance indicators, methods of measurement and ways of forming a judgement. If a product or performance indicator is defined unambiguously, without tolerating variety, it is very likely to have little legitimacy.

It may be added that many organizations also have to report in multiple ways. Suppose a municipality is obliged to report to central government, its own municipal council and its citizens and clients. Each may demand different requirements from the municipality, which may lead to multiple product definitions, performance indicators and methods of measurement and forming a judgement. Multiple reporting may therefore also demand tolerance of variety: multiple reporting relationships use – for example – multiple product definitions. A metaphor of a statue and floodlights may be applied here. Illuminating the statue from several different perspectives creates a different image each time. Each image is correct, but a single perspective always gives a distorted image. Variety is also beneficial to the substance of performance measurement and contributes to the legitimacy of performance measurement.

If a single-value, questionable, product definition is chosen for a product that is difficult to define, a possible consequence is that the performance measurement will have no legitimacy, or will lead to perversion. If it should appear that multiple product definitions each yield the same image from the performance measurement, this image will consequently be more legitimate. Conversely, should the image yielded by each product definition be different, then it will be evident that no unambiguous image of an organization's performance is possible, and the organization's management will have to accept that fact.

4 Design principle 3: Dynamics

It is important for performance measurement to be a lively and challenging activity, because it must be able to cope with the dynamism that is involved in creating products and services. There are two aspects to this requirement: performance measurement must illuminate (1) the process of creating products, and (2) the dynamism in product development.

A feature of the previous two design principles is that they remain within the performance measurement paradigm: a professional organization delivers products and services and must be assessed on its output. In addition, performance measurement may address the *professional process* of creating the performance. The process of creation is concerned with such questions as what effort is expended by an organization, how innovative it is, how it copes with constantly changing surroundings, which activities it gives priority to, and how it maintains the relationship with third parties that are able to influence its performance. No justice can be done to an organization that keeps its production figures stable under difficult circumstances, in the face of numerous innovations in the process of creating the products, with a single product measurement. Although the production remains unchanged, the process of creation has changed drastically.

Performance measurement that addresses only products is blind to dynamism in the processes and will be dull and static. While there may be considerable dynamism in the organization – new processes, innovation, new challenges, new people – attention remains fixed on production figures, which, as stated above, always gives a limited view of performance.

A second aspect is the necessary attention to changes that may occur in the assessment of an organization's products. Under the influence of new political priorities, developments in the environment of one professional organization or innovations in the primary process, existing product definitions may become outdated and need replacing with new ones. Allowing freedom for these changes makes performance management a lively activity.

Chapter 5

Trust and interaction

1 Introduction

Performance measurement can widen the gap between manager and professional, as Chapter 3 explains. The Law of Decreasing Effectiveness can emerge and performance measurement can degenerate into a ritual. This is why it is desirable at various crucial moments in the performance measurement process to arrange for *interaction* between management and professional. Interaction helps build trust between the two parties and in the performance measurement system.[1]

It goes without saying that interaction plays a role in the *design* of a performance measurement system. Professionals may be invited to say what constitutes a good product definition and what they want to be assessed on. If management and professionals then arrive at product definitions and performance indicators by mutual agreement, there is a greater chance that they will be taken seriously, which will help them fulfil their function.

Once a system exists, interaction will then also play an important role in its *use*.

Some form of interaction is called for in reaching decisions on the following subjects:

- The first issue is to identify the *functions* of performance measurement and the intended *forums* for dealing with the performance measurement results. The design principle of interaction means here that neither management nor the professional is allowed unilaterally to change the functions or forums of performance measurement. Once performance measurement has a function and a forum, then the manager and professional can trust that any deviation from it will demand a form of consultation. A unilateral accumulation of functions or forums is also detrimental to trust in the system (Section 2). What, moreover, is the relationship between the production delivered by the professional and the associated judgement reached by the manager? Section 3 asserts that a judgement should always be formed in interaction between the manager and the professional. If not, and the manager forms a judgement without consultation, then the perverse effect on performance measurement will be strong.

These aspects of the principle of interaction are beneficial to the trust that *professionals* in particular have in performance measurement. The trust of *managers* in performance measurement may also be enhanced:

- In layered organizations in particular, decentralized professional units often have their own forms of performance measurement. The risk from the manager's perspective is that the incentives assumed in decentralized performance measurement may conflict with those assumed in central performance measurement. The design principle of interaction implies that the manager and the professional unit enter into agreements on the freedom allowed for decentralized performance measurement to deviate from central performance measurement (Section 4). This is the realm of the 'boundary spanner', who resides on the interface between the management and professional systems (Section 5).
- Finally, performance is reported by the professional unit. An important question is whether the performance reported is consistent with reality. From a manager's perspective, some degree of monitoring of the reporting is desirable. The most effective is a form of soft monitoring, which is shaped interactively (Section 6).

2 Be clear about the functions and forums

If performance indicators yield only partial information, the first rule of the game is for management and the professional to enter into agreements on the *functions* of the figures and on the *forums* for which they are intended.[2] The point in reaching agreements on the functions is the question of what the production figures will be used for. Are they intended only to create transparency? Is any financial reward attached? Or are they used as a benchmark? The point in reaching agreements on forums is the question of who has access to the figures and is entitled to use them. Are the figures only for internal use? Or will parties outside the organization also get to see them? Will they be published, or will they be kept confidential?

In the absence of agreements on the above issues, perversion of a system is likely. What could happen is that the professional becomes very suspicious of the way in which performance measurement will be used. The professional submits the figures to management, but is unaware of which other actors will see them, and how the figures will be used. Gaming the numbers is then a strategy of avoiding the risk of figures being used wrongly.

A psychotherapist has discussion sessions with a patient, the costs of which are paid by an insurance company. The insurance company asks for various details as justification of the bill. The psychotherapist has to complete a check-list to identify the patient's problems, including the nature of the disorder, whether the patient has a criminal record and if he or she has relational problems. The psychotherapist also has to state the number of sessions that were needed to complete the therapy.

The *function* of this information is to justify the bill. The *forum* that is to use the information is the insurance company. It is evident that the information given by the psychotherapist is rather poor. No additional information is provided about the disorder; one therapist will tick many items, while another will be reticent when completing the form; the number of sessions means little without also stating the nature of the treatment; one patient is more amenable than another and may require fewer sessions.

Suppose now that the insurance company changes the function, such that the information is to serve not only to justify the bill, but also for setting standards. The insurance company will analyse the claim forms submitted and unilaterally determine a limit to the number of sessions, for example for a patient with characteristics x, y and z. The insurance company will not reimburse more than a given number of sessions.

This change of function can lead to perverse behaviour. The psychotherapists may well now complete the forms in such a way that more of their sessions are paid for, even if the picture presented by the form is not entirely consistent with the patient's clinical picture. Psychotherapists who do not do so may be caught in the middle between the insurance company and the patient and will feel extremely unfairly treated, to the detriment of the relationship with the insurance company. Neither is the unilateral change ultimately in the interest of the insurance company, because a reality-on-paper may be created that has nothing to do with the real world of therapist and patient, and which may also cost the insurance company even more money. Suppose that an insurance company wishes to change the standard in line with the new figures. This would be an extremely risky step, because the figures will have been perverted by the unilateral function change and will therefore be unreliable.

This is not to say that the information on the claim form can never be used in setting standards. However, the unilateral change of the function of the figures, without consulting the suppliers of those figures, can lead to these perverse effects.

Something similar applies to changing the *forum*. Suppose these figures will be used not only by insurance companies but also by policy-makers, for example in the future allocation of financial resources. Here, too, it is risky for the user to cite weak figures in policy development; it may be an incentive for the professional for perverse behaviour.

A second rule of the game follows from the example of the psychotherapist. Neither management nor the professional may unilaterally change the function and forums of performance measurement. A rule of the game of this kind creates predictability and is beneficial to trust in the system and to the mutual trust between the manager and the professional.

A third rule of the game is that it is sensible to limit the number of functions and forums. An accumulation of functions and forums causes the following mechanism to operate:

- every function and every forum elicits its own forms of positive effects;
- every function and every forum elicits its own forms of perverse effects;
- the function with the highest impact invokes the Law of Decreasing Effectiveness, because this function creates strong incentives for perverse behaviour;
- this leads to perverted information;
- which is then used in the other functions;
- in the course of time, an accumulation of functions and forums thus leads to an accumulation of perverse effects.

To the above may be added the point that a system which has to fulfil a large number of functions simultaneously may fossilize. If performance measurement has a number of different functions, the same product definitions have to be used to serve each of them. However, it is perfectly conceivable for a product to call for different definitions to serve different functions.

My university, the Delft University of Technology, operates a system of output funding: a faculty's research budget is determined partly by the production of articles, in which a distinction is drawn between academic and professional publications. Academic publications are for academic peers, whereas professional publications are for a broader public and are often more application-oriented. A list of the faculty's academic and professional production is submitted each year to the Board, which is then able to allocate the research funds.

The research in my faculty is reviewed regularly by external parties, who compare my faculty's academic and professional production and that of other faculties in the same specialization at other universities. Is it possible that the same production figures are used? Absolutely not. Delft uses definitions of 'academic publication' and 'professional publication' that are generally compatible with the specializations at this university. The external review uses definitions that are compatible with the specific specialization. For instance, the Delft definition of 'academic publication' is far stricter than the one used in my specialization. My specialization is, for example, highly application-oriented and therefore ascribes a higher value than the TU Delft to publications in the national language. Anyone unaware of a distinction of this kind will be at a serious disadvantage in any comparison between faculties based on a specialization.

Suppose a third party produces a ranking of universities relying heavily on the number of academic publications per staff member. This is a third function and forum. This ranking of universities requires the comparison of a spectrum of specializations that is wider than the range on offer at my university, or required for an external review. This forum may therefore require yet another definition of 'academic publication'.

Problems therefore quickly arise in producing cut-and-dried definitions in the case of an accumulation of functions or forums, in that they will simply be incompatible with the multiple functions or forums and therefore need constant adjustment.

This example clearly illustrates how pointless it is to endeavour to achieve a comprehensive system (in the sense of being suitable for all functions and forums). An alternative is a more moderate position: limited functions for a restricted number of forums. For the professional this creates trust that the figures have limited meaning, thereby doing justice to the complexity of the primary process. This in turn will be beneficial to the trust between the manager and the professional, while also supplying the manager with more reliable information.

3 Limit the impact of performance measurement; no direct link between production, forming a judgement and impact

Chapter 3 discussed the Law of Decreasing Effectiveness: when performance measurement has a high impact, the perverse effects increase, and the effectiveness of performance measurement correspondingly decreases. This law can in the worst case operate in concert with other laws. Mushrooming occurs, collective blindness sets in, systems become rituals and perverted systems continue to be used regardless. Two rules of the game counteract these laws.

Limited impact

The first rule of the game is that the impact of performance measurement must always be restricted. If a large part of the budget or reputation, or the degrees of freedom of a professional organization depend on the quantified performance, a system will become perverted.

The question that immediately arises is what constitutes a high impact? If part of the budget depends on the output, is the dividing line at 40 per cent, 20 per cent or 5 per cent? Of course, there is no correct answer. Even if it is evident that a small proportion of a budget is dependent on output, the professionals may perceive a high impact, for example because the professionals have little slack in the budget and additional funds are urgently needed, or because they are simply unaware of what proportion of the budget depends on output.

The answer to the question of what constitutes a high impact can therefore be answered only in a process of interaction between management and professional in which they can compare their perceptions of the system's impact. Subjects that might be raised in this process are views on the impact among professionals, views on the positive and perverse effects and the question of whether the laws are already manifesting themselves. Both the manager and the professional can form a view. If consensus exists, the system can be structured in accordance with that consensus. If the manager and the professional do not share the same opinion, then the manager will have to take his or her own decision. The process of interaction that leads up to this decision will guarantee that the manager has the best possible information (see Section 5 for the requirements that the above imposes on the manager).

Indirect link

Suppose now that the manager and the professional disagree on what the correct impact is. Or suppose that the impact is actually high. Yet another rule of the game is relevant in this situation: there should be an indirect link between output figures and their impact.

A direct link means that for a given production, the judgement and the impact are 'self-executing'.

- The performance indicator for a police force is the number of written bookings per year. Each district must produce a predetermined number of bookings per year per officer. The production will be calculated at the end of the year. The police force management team announces at the beginning of a year that a production below level x will be considered to be an under-performance (direct judgement). The performance of the districts will be published, which is a form of naming and shaming (direct impact).
- The performance indicator for a university is the number of published academic articles. An amount is paid for each article published. A faculty's research budget in a budget year consists of the number of articles published

in the previous year multiplied by a predetermined amount per article. A direct link means that a faculty knows directly at the time of submitting its production figures what the judgement will be (the faculty either did or did not meet the targets) and likewise what the financial impact will be (the level of funding in the following year).

The advantage of a direct link is that it can be a strong incentive for performance. A direct link can be useful, in particular when an organization has lost all orientation to output, and is entirely inwardly focused (i.e. on throughput). It can help prompt an organization to refocus on results. But, as mentioned above, a direct link can also invoke the Law of Decreasing Effectiveness (see Chapter 3). A direct link can moreover have negative consequences for a manager. Once a direct link exists, the manager is bound to it. The manager can become a prisoner of his or her own system. It could be that one of the better district heads achieves poor figures, or that a strategically important faculty publishes so little that it is forced to phase out part of its research.

Where an indirect link exists between production, forming a judgement and reward, the judgement and reward to which a certain production will lead are also indicated in advance.

However, the link between these three factors is not 'self-executing'. Determining the production, forming the judgement and imposing sanctions are separate, and there is always some room for manoeuvre between these three activities. The judgement is formed only after the manager and the professional have exchanged their insights on the performance. If output is low, the question that arises is *why* is it low? Was it caused by sloppy management, carefully considered professional choices for other priorities, or external circumstances? This shifts the attention away from performance measurement as an instrument for a unilateral assessment to performance measurement as an instrument for a joint assessment.[3]

I again use the example of the rat catcher. When the rat catcher reports that few rats have been caught, several explanations are possible. Sloppy management: the rat catcher went on holiday just at the time when rats are usually caught, without arranging for a replacement. A carefully considered professional choice: the number of rats in the area has declined so sharply that catching even more could make the future population too strong and resistant. Other priorities: the rat catcher was occupied with other unforeseen tasks that were more urgent than catching rats.

The rat catcher may put forward these and similar arguments. In the light of the view the manager subsequently forms, he or she arrives at a judgement. This means that the professional still has some freedom. The axe will not fall immediately after the production is determined, but as a professional he or she can still put forward technical arguments for sub-standard production. Indirect links thus moderate incentives for perverse behaviour, in that the professional still has an opportunity to influence the judgement after the performance. This is beneficial to his or her trust in the system and in the manager.

Finally, an indirect link provides an opportunity to discuss the consequences to be linked to a production figure. An organization that performs well may be rewarded financially, but other forms of reward exist. For instance, it is conceivable that the professionals are granted greater autonomy in exchange for good performance. In a process of interaction, the professionals may be asked to identify the subjects on which they would like to have additional degrees of freedom.[4] The impact of a good performance may then be high (many extra degrees of freedom), but because it is not an automatic mechanism, and may even be unknown in advance, the operation of the Law of Decreasing Effectiveness will be less strong.

Indirect links are necessary, but also entail a significant risk. They may lure the manager into arbitrary behaviour. A reward per product is agreed in advance, but the indirect link allows the manager to back out after the event. For the professional this means that the consequences of his or her performance are unpredictable.

Again, this risk may be averted by agreeing a number of clear *rules of the game* on the *process* to be followed from determining the performance to forming a judgement. Suppose, for example, that the following simple rule of the game applies in this process: 'Management consults with the professionals on the performance before forming a judgement on the performance; if the management judgement differs from that of the professionals, supporting arguments will be given.'

A rule of the game of this kind 'forces' the manager to listen to the professional when forming a judgement. However, he or she is also free to differ from the professional's perception of the performance, but then has to provide supporting arguments. The idea with this rule of the game, and in particular the duty to provide arguments, is to reduce the chance of managerial arbitrariness.

In summary, the reasoning is as follows:

- a direct link is avoided;
- instead there is an indirect link, which offers both the manager and the professional freedom in forming the judgement and the reward, which

is necessary because performance measurement never entirely does justice to professional activities;

- the risk of an indirect link is that it leads to managerial arbitrariness;
- therefore a clear course of the proceedings is agreed, from determining the production, through forming the judgement to setting the reward. This course of the proceedings counters the risks of a soft link.

4 Provide scope for attenuating the incentive of performance measurement; tolerate a decentralized incentive structure that differs from the central incentive structure

An important issue in the design of performance measurement is deciding the layer to which the incentive arising from performance measurement should be perceptible. Suppose a central layer in an organization defines a product, indicating that there will be a reward on realizing a certain production level. This financial incentive is then communicated to, for example, a decentralized layer, which in turn passes on the incentive to a layer below. Can this incentive also be passed on down to an individual professional? Doing so would tell him or her exactly which products would produce which financial reward: if a production level of bookings, court rulings, orders, publications and suchlike is realized, he or she could calculate how much money he or she is generating for the organization. A following question is whether the decentralized incentive structure should be allowed to differ from the structure that was designed centrally. If it is arranged centrally so that products x and y are to be rewarded, is it acceptable on a decentralized layer for the products y and z be rewarded? Or for the reward for x and y to be halved, and the budget thus freed up to be distributed in accordance with entirely different criteria?

Tolerance for attenuation of the incentive and for a decentralized incentive structure: a dilemma

The above questions again demand a qualified answer. The literature often warns against passing financial incentives right down to the layer of individual personnel.[5]

In the first place, performance measurement can lead to perverse effects, and these effects are at a maximum if the incentive applies at the level of the individual. If a production objective is imposed on the lowest layer in the organization – the individual professional – then the implication is that everything and everyone in the organization is subject to the performance measurement system. This may be evaluated in two ways:

- *positively*: the incentives for the favourable effects of performance measurement are maximized;
- *negatively*: the incentives for the perverse effects of performance measurement are maximized.

In the second place, the literature refers repeatedly to the fact that performance indicators which are perceptible on an individual level are often threatening to the individual professional. Professionals who perform tasks that are crucial but difficult to quantify will achieve poor scores in an individualized system of performance measurement. This situation gives performance measurement a negative connotation, making it very tempting to pervert the system. But here, too, if an organization has fallen into decline, a – temporary – individualized incentive structure may also be considered in a positive light.

Both considerations lead to the same conclusion: the decentralized management must form an opinion, in interaction with the professionals, of the effects of individualized performance measurement and then decide on whether a performance measurement should be passed down to the individual professional. Some scope must always exist for attenuating the incentive somewhere between the central layer and the individual professional.

However, the incentive can be so strongly attenuated as to lose the benefits of performance measurement. This is a common phenomenon in organizations and suggests a second scenario:

- a performance measurement system is introduced;
- it must then be implemented on a number of layers;
- the incentive is attenuated on one or more of the layers, so that it is no longer perceptible on the layer where the performance has to be delivered.

A phenomenon that is closely related to this issue is that a decentralized professional unit sometimes develops its own incentive structure, which may deviate from the incentive structure in the central performance measurement system. This situation may be undesirable, in that two contradictory incentive structures are in use. The controlling effect of performance measurement could consequently be lost. However, a professional unit can also have sound arguments for attenuating certain central incentives:

- the system is refined and still leads only to perverse effects;
- the professionals perform well even without an incentive structure;
- innovation is necessary, but it will not be brought about with the central incentive structure;

- crucial activities produce poor scores in the performance measurement system and are therefore likely to be undervalued.

By developing a decentralised incentive structure, justice can be done to the special circumstances in which the decentralized unit finds itself. Performance measurement can have favourable effects precisely because it deviates from the central incentive structure, which implies a dilemma in this case too. Deviation, like attenuation, can be considered positively and negatively. The above gives rise to the following picture surrounding this dilemma:

- There are two dilemmas: allowing incentives to propagate versus attenuating incentives, and prohibiting a decentralized incentive structure versus tolerating a decentralized incentive structure.
- It is difficult and unwise for a manager on a central layer to prescribe *ex ante* and with binding force what form the decentralized incentive structure should take.
- A rule of the game is produced instead: the decentralized unit may attenuate and may deviate, but must provide supporting arguments for how and where it intends to attenuate the incentives and which deviations it will make from the central model.
- The central layer can later form an opinion, giving its reasons.
- Agreements can also be made on the 'burden of proof'. A possible agreement could be for the central layer to accept in principle the professional unit's arguments, unless they are found to be patently incorrect or unreasonable. This introduces a test of the reasonableness of the arguments. The burden of proof in deviating from the arguments resides with the central layer. Of course, the agreement could equally put the burden of proof with respect to arguments for attenuating or deviating on to the decentralized unit.

5 The importance of the managing professional as boundary spanner between management and profession

The sections above refer consistently to 'the' managers and 'the' professionals. Many choices demand interaction between management and professionals:

- deciding for which functions and forums production figures are intended;
- deciding when the impact of performance measurement is considered to be too high;

- forming a judgement on a professional's output;
- determining how much an incentive may be attenuated;
- forming a judgement on the effects of a decentralized incentive structure.

A managerial perspective is possible on each of these choices, in which values such as uniformity, consistency and completeness will have an important place: not too many different product definitions, not too many changes to existing systems, not too much freedom for decentralized units. There is also a professional perspective, in which values such as variety, dynamism and diversity will play an important role: tolerate multiple product definitions if professions differ, adapt systems if they squeeze the professional, and allow freedom for decentralized units.

Given these different perspectives, there is a natural risk that interaction between management and professionals will lead only to conflict and not to forming a common view. There is a managerial system and a professional system, which speak different languages and uphold different values, and which are difficult to unite. Chapter 3 discussed in depth the effect of this situation in terms of the ritualization of performance measurement.

The implication of this analysis is that it is highly important to identify the actors in an organization who reside on the boundary between the managerial and professional systems. The actors concerned can both play the managerial game and fully comprehend the profession. An actor with these qualities will be close enough to the professional process to be able to understand and influence it, and close enough to the managerial layer to understand and do justice to its values.

This boundary spanner can thus often be best placed to weigh the managerial and professional interests against each other. He or she is able to translate managerial interventions for the professional layer; for example, by making quantified objectives set by management meaningful to professionals and preventing these objectives from resulting only in strategic behaviour. He or she is able to translate professional experience and performance for the managerial layer and to present the information in such a way that management will not interpret the performance too simplistically. The boundary spanner does have to be given the necessary freedom, by both the manager and professionals.

- The boundary spanner needs freedom to make the central incentives meaningful and substantial for the professionals. An incentive in a police force that rewards bookings has little meaning. If the incentive is translated down to the individual professional, it is likely that many pointless bookings will result. The boundary spanner can make this incentive meaningful by translating it into objectives that are consistent with the specific circumstances of the professional unit concerned. It goes without saying that this endeavour will be possible only if he or she has the necessary freedom.

- The boundary spanner also needs the freedom to contribute to reporting to management. The professionals will have to give him or her this freedom, for example in the form of a willingness to align performance with high managerial priorities (and possibly a low professional priority).
- The boundary spanner is excellently placed to answer the question of what constitutes a desirable decentralized incentive structure. Indeed, in answering this question, he or she must take into account the managerial value that performance measurement must have a stimulating effect and must be as complete and consistent as possible, while also doing justice to a professional unit's specific characteristics.

The boundary spanner's position on the boundary between management and the profession theoretically gives him or her the power to commit both management and the profession. This *managing professional* knows the profession, but also knows how to play the managerial game. The managing professional is sometimes treated with a degree of disdain in traditional professional organizations. From the manager's perspective he or she is someone merely half-way through the development process from professional to manager. From the professional's perspective he or she is someone who has turned his or her back on the profession to do management's dirty work. In reality, managing professionals can occupy key positions in professional organizations, sometimes with more commitment power (i.e. the power to commit an organization) than the administrative layers above them.

6 Turn monitoring into an interactive process

When professional organizations are rewarded on the basis of performance, the implication is that their products have a high value (in terms of money or reputation), which can lead to many forms of strategic behaviour and necessitate monitoring of output. This monitoring can be given a unilateral form. The manager monitors whether the performance has been delivered. For example, hard copies of academic publications are requested to determine whether they were actually published and may be counted as an academic publication (universities). A list is required of schoolchildren who were absent from a test (schools). If it should turn out that a drop in the number of decisions not to prosecute was because police bookings were no longer being forwarded to the Public Prosecution

Service, the Ministry of Justice requests figures on the number of police bookings (Public Prosecution Service) alongside the figures on the number of decisions not to prosecute.

However, unilateral monitoring of this kind has some significant disadvantages.

First, monitoring can be extremely labour-intensive. Any form of monitoring may potentially lead to new strategic behaviour. Furthermore, unilateral monitoring does not give the professionals joint responsibility for the monitoring. It is a situation of the monitor versus the professional which can result in a cat-and-mouse game, and therefore in incentives for more and new strategic behaviour.

Second, strategic behaviour often permits an ambiguous interpretation. If the Public Prosecution Service reviews the bookings at the police station, decides not to forward certain bookings and so reduces the number of decisions not to prosecute, is that strategic behaviour? Or is it a legitimate form of working in a chain? If a researcher's publications are always on the same theme, is that perverse behaviour (no innovation) or a legitimate attempt to disseminate academic knowledge as far as possible? Behind unilateral monitoring lies the assumption that clear meanings can be given to behaviour of this kind.

Third, behind unilateral monitoring is the assumption that a performance measurement system relates simply to the real world: the definitions are unambiguous and easy to apply. As mentioned several times, the professional reality is often more complex than the simplicity of a performance measurement system.

'Professional education institutes and universities submit "unreliable" figures on the number of students leaving educational programmes with a degree. These study yield figures are calculated in various different ways. . . . Some educational programmes do not count students who drop out in the first year in the study yield, while others do. One faculty may count "entrants" with a university of professional education (HBO) certificate, who are entitled to skip the first university year, in the figures, thus raising the first year yield relative to other educational programmes. The average study duration is also stated only for graduates, so ignoring drop-outs. . . . The Association of Universities in the Netherlands has a guideline for calculating yield statistics. . . . The Association says that it understands that "faculties find it hard to adhere to the guideline. . . . They are confronted with students who are enrolled in two degree programmes, but who pay only one set of tuition fees, or with students who attend hardly any lectures, if at all, and therefore drop out" [known as phantom entrants, who tend to lower the yield but are completely outside the faculty's control].'[6]

If these assumptions do not apply, monitoring will also have to be an interactive process. Interactive monitoring prevents the cat-and-mouse game surrounding strategic behaviour. It instead means setting a thief to catch a thief. It is necessary because professionals' behaviour allows different interpretations and because a single definition of a product may conceal totally different realities. Strict monitoring of production would lead to patent unfairness and would seriously erode a system's legitimacy. Another of the many performance measurement paradoxes is revealed: adhering strictly to formal product definitions undermines the legitimacy of the system.

Interaction is oriented primarily to achieving authoritative monitoring. It is harder for professionals to shirk this responsibility when determining the production of a joint activity.

Second, monitoring is then also a learning process. Experience gained in the monitoring process may be used, for example, for improving the system. The professionals can disseminate their experience in the organization, possibly curtailing future strategic behaviour.

Third, it creates a joint view of what is and is not acceptable behaviour. The above example of the yield figures illustrates how important this is. Are we dealing with an innocent form of creative bookkeeping? Or with fraud? Or with well-intentioned professionals struggling with unworkable systems? If management has no sense of the complexity of the real world behind the simple performance measurement system, there will come a time when it is unpleasantly surprised by the practices professionals then start to engage in. If professionals are insufficiently sensitive to the function given by management to a performance measurement system, there is a chance that they will use the system excessively and exhibit too much strategic behaviour.

Chapter 6

Content and variety

I Introduction

Performance measurement easily becomes a weak activity, and is meaningful only when performance is viewed from various perspectives, because justice is then done to the multiple valued nature of the professional's products and services. Variety, then, is an important design principle, which may be elaborated in three ways:

- When production figures are available, the next question is who is *able to give meaning to the figures*; in other words, who has 'meaning-making rights'? Variety means that there is no monopoly on giving meaning, and that multiple interpretations of production figures are allowed (Section 2).
- The use of multiple product definitions is necessary, but matters can be taken one step further if an organization tolerates *conflicting product definitions* to make a performance visible in multiple, competing ways. This aspect is discussed in Section 3.
- Finally, variety also contrasts with *comprehensiveness*. Comprehensiveness means that an organization's entire performance is measured, and is therefore incorporated into a comprehensive performance measurement system. The principle of variety means differentiation between types of products and that an organization then tolerates these products each playing a different (and sometimes no) role in the performance measurement system (Section 4).

2 Giving meaning: no monopoly on 'meaning-making rights'

An important issue in performance measurement is *which* interpretation and meaning should be given to the figures, and who has the 'meaning-making rights': *who* gives meaning to the statistics? These issues are of great importance. If an incorrect meaning takes root, the consequences can be serious. A manager may base policy decisions on the wrong interpretation. The Law of Collective Blindness may manifest itself. The behaviour of the professional may also be influenced undesirably. Publications of mortality rates that are interpreted incorrectly may tend to discourage cardiologists from performing risky operations.[1]

Suppose a police force management team reports a rise in the crime detection percentage in its district. What does that say about the performance of the police? Or if a hospital reports a fall in the mortality rate, what does that say about the hospital's performance? And what does a drop in the number of acts of violence in a prison say about the performance of the prison governor?

Only one answer is possible to questions of this kind: the figures say nothing about the performance. A sensible judgement on the police, the hospital and the prison governor is possible only after the figures have been interpreted and meaning given to them. I provide two examples to show how meaningless a production figure is.

Example 1: mortality rate

It is common in many Western countries to publish hospitals' mortality rates: the number of patients who die in the hospital, which may be expressed as various ratios (e.g. a percentage of the total number of patients, or of the number of medical treatments).

The meaning of a figure of this kind is extremely limited and cannot be interpreted without knowing the reality behind the figure. I give a few examples:[2]

- Mortality rates in rural Scotland are higher than in England. The reason is that patients have a longer journey to hospital and therefore arrive in a poorer condition.
- Low mortality rates may result from shorter hospitalization periods, because patients are discharged to die at home and are thus not counted in the figures.
- The nature of treatments such as oncology has changed considerably. Patients are now treated in hospital and then return home, reporting at a later date for another session. An uninterrupted stay in hospital is therefore a thing of the past. If a patient dies, it is a matter of chance whether this happens in hospital or at home. If the patient should happen to die while in hospital, the death will be incorporated into the mortality rate, but not if the patient dies at home.

- As medical knowledge advances, patients who once would have been deemed untreatable are now admitted. The mortality rate among these patients will be higher than among other patients, almost by definition.
- Some hospitals collaborate with hospices in offering terminal care to patients. Collaboration of this kind will depress a hospital's mortality rate.

The essence of these examples is that the mortality rate is influenced by many factors and not only by the quality of the medical treatment. If a mortality rate falls drastically, it may be a sign of higher-quality medical treatment. However, other explanations are equally possible.

Example 2: acts of violence against prison staff

Suppose a Parliament has concerns about prison conditions. One of the main aspects of concern is the number of acts of violence against prison staff. The Ministry of Justice publishes the figures shown in Table 6.1.

The figures show how much violence is committed against prison staff. They also show how often a sanction is imposed on prisoners – solitary confinement in a punishment cell. If Parliament's aim is the lowest possible number of acts of violence, which prison performs better and why? Very many answers are possible to this question.

- *Interpretation 1 is that B performs better.* The number of acts of violence is significantly lower than at A. The reason is that B imposes more sanctions. The interpretation would hold that a prison imposing sanctions is rewarded with fewer acts of violence.
- *Interpretation 2 is that A performs better.* With only twenty-six sanctions, A has managed to reduce the number of acts of violence to ten, whereas B needed

Table 6.1 Acts of violence against staff and sanctions in two prisons

	Prison A	Prison B
Acts of violence against staff, per 100 occupied cells	10	2
Solitary confinements in punishment cell, per 100 occupied cells	26	161
Written complaints against solitary confinement, per 100 cells	13	3
Number of prisoners registered for solitary confinement, per 100 cells	0	18

to impose almost seven times as many sanctions, but the number of acts of violence is only five times fewer.

- *Interpretation 3 is that B performs better.* Prison A receives many written complaints from prisoners against the sanctions. Prison B receives far fewer written complaints. Conclusion: it is evident that prison B manages to provide arguments for the sanctions that are accepted by the prisoners, even though many more sanctions are imposed than at A. Many accepted sanctions (B) is a far better performance than a few unaccepted sanctions (A).

- *Interpretation 4 is that A performs better.* The large number of written complaints shows how difficult the prisoners are. Even so, few sanctions are imposed. The number of acts of violence is higher than at B, but in view of the difficult nature of the prisoners, interpretation 2 has even more merit.

- *Interpretation 5 is that A performs better.* The national placement committee is constantly confronted with prison B's refusal to accept prisoners. Furthermore, as soon as prisoners commit any violence, prison B puts them forward for transfer to another prison. Prison A accepts any prisoner and sees it as a matter of professional honour not to put them forward for transfer. The logical consequence of this attitude is that the number of acts of violence is higher than at B.

- *Interpretation 6 is that the figures cannot be compared.* Prison B has an austere regime, which means that many prisoners are kept in their cells, resulting in fewer acts of violence. Prison A has a normal regime and therefore more acts of violence.

- *Interpretation 7 is that the figures cannot be compared.* The policy in prison A is for infrequent but long-term placements. The idea is that this policy has the greatest deterrent effect. Prison B's policy, conversely, is for short placements, sometimes for only a couple of hours.

- *Interpretation 8 is that the figures cannot be compared.* Prison A is more decentralized than B, which means that a departmental head can order solitary confinement without permission from the governor (provided the prisoner consents). However, the figures report only the solitary confinements ordered by the governor. The order is always given by the governor in prison B.

- *Interpretation 9 is that the figures cannot be compared.* The soft and hard drugs policies of the prisons differ considerably. The possession or use of drugs is punished in prison B by solitary confinement, leading to relatively many solitary confinements. The solitary confinements have to do not only with acts of violence, but also with the drugs policy. The figures therefore have an extremely limited meaning for forming a judgement on acts of violence and related sanctions.

This example clarifies a number of matters:

- Countless conflicting interpretations of the figures are possible.
- An interpretation based exclusively on the figures for acts of violence and sanctions (interpretations 1 and 2) will be extremely poor.
- Additional figures, on the number of written complaints or the number of transfers, provides a clearer picture (interpretations 3, 4 and 5), but it remains poor compared with interpretations 6 to 9.
- Contradictory interpretations and meanings can be given based on the same figures (interpretations 3 and 4).
- A richer picture is produced in interpretations 6 to 9, but they too demand considerable effort in putting the meaning of the figures into perspective. The figures do not express the prison's performance with regard to acts of violence, but entirely different matters.

If a meaning is constructed based exclusively on the figures from the performance measurement, the meaning will at best be poor and probably wrong. Production figures can at most be a 'trigger' for forming a more detailed view of acts of violence. Performance measurement is not fitted with 'dials' (scales from which performance can be read), but only 'tin-openers', which invite further investigation.[3] The idea is that anyone with performance measurement at their disposal can use it to form an initial view of performance and identify aspects calling for more qualitative information. Performance measurement gives no answers, but rather provides inspiration for asking the right questions.[4]

Because multiple, partly conflicting, interpretations are possible, it is important that giving meaning is not a monopoly. Having a monopoly means that (1) one actor decides (2) which figures are relevant, and (3) the interpretation and meaning to be attached to these figures. Monopoly is countered by having variety as a rule of the game: freedom for a variety of meanings must be allowed in interpreting the figures. I elaborate this rule of the game below, but first discuss the risk of a monopoly on giving meaning.

If there is insufficient freedom for creating a variety of meanings, the consequence is not only poor meanings, but possibly also that the interpretation of the figures is driven by mechanisms other than the reality behind the figures.

- *The first meaning institutionalizes.* Giving meaning has an important temporal component. Robin Tolmach Lakoff pointed out that the first meaning to arise often survives longest. It acquires the status of 'common sense', and changing or replacing this meaning is far from simple.[5] This situation can do much harm, in particular because the most obvious interpretation, based on limited figures, is not always the right one (see the acts of violence example). For the professional, institution-alization of a poor interpretation is harmful if a meaning that takes root with a manager does no justice to the reality behind the figure, but none the less determines the direction of policy development. The corres-ponding situation for the manager is if the meaning that takes root conceals professional failure to perform.

- *The outlier is the deviation.* This implies that attention is paid only to performance that deviates (from the standard, from the historical trend, or from the performance of other organizations). Performance that does not deviate does not demand to be given a meaning. This kind of thinking is risky in that similar performances may conceal different realities. Using the acts of violence example, if prison C were also to be considered, with figures that closely resemble those of B, two risks occur. The first is that it may be concluded that the performance of B and C is normal and that of A is the exception. The second is that it may be concluded that B and C not only have the same figures, but that they can also be interpreted similarly: the reality behind the figures is pre-sumed to be the same.

- *The meaning that reflects existing preferences institutionalizes.* A third mechanism is that the meaning results from the preferences of man-agers and professionals. Suppose the management of a hospital attaches great importance to reducing waiting lists. Suppose that, according to the performance measurement system, the waiting lists indeed become shorter, confirming management's preference. The incentive to seek out different explanations – which might lead to the conclusion that perverse effects are at work – may be extremely small in a situation of this kind. Monopolization of giving meaning is lying in wait with the explanation that the reduction in waiting lists is genuine and that patient care has therefore improved.

Prohibiting the monopolization of giving meaning therefore serves not only to prevent giving poor meanings, but also to prevent institution-alizing a meaning, focusing attention exclusively on the 'outliers', or allowing the meaning to be a function of managerial preferences.[6] This necessary variety can be guaranteed by making rules of the game in which actors are involved in giving meaning to which figures and how they will interact.

Variety ensures that meaning-giving is a process in which multiple meanings compete with each other. The result may be an unambiguous meaning, but it is just as probable that different actors have different opinions on the interpretation of the figures. Variety has a number of benefits:

- If a meaning ultimately emerges from the variety and is accepted by all concerned, it is very likely that it will be richer than the original meanings from these actors, and the meaning will moreover carry more authority.
- If there is disagreement between managers and professionals, or among individual professionals, regarding the meaning of the figures, it may be reason for further investigation, which may be extraordinarily valuable and contribute to learning processes both for management and professionals. A Dutch training hospital reported an increase in the heart unit's mortality rate in 2006. The hospital's first interpretation was that high mortality is inherent in the training hospital's role, because a training hospital carries out more complex operations than a normal hospital. In response to disagreement on this interpretation – in this case between the inspectors and the hospital – the matter was investigated further, revealing an entirely different meaning: poor organization and too many conflicts between the surgeons.[7]
- The fact that management and professionals do not arrive at a single meaning, and that the various meanings are contradictory, is also important. For instance, the situation may lead to restraint in formulating policy that conflicts with one of the meanings and where there are possible irreversible consequences.
- If both the manager and the professional are given an opportunity to provide their meaning for the figures, it gives them freedom, which can be a disincentive for perverse behaviour. If professionals are denied the opportunity to give their own interpretation to the figures, they may find performance measurement threatening. If so, it might incentivize perverse behaviour.

3 Allow freedom for variety in product definitions and performance indicators; no comprehensive performance measurement, no unambiguous performance measurement

The literature often has recommendations based on the idea that performance measurement should be a comprehensive system.

- 'The product budget defines *all* [italics added] activities of the municipalities in terms of products [output] or effects [outcome]. . . . The product budget is completely consistent with other policy and management instruments.'[8]
- 'The objectives [i.e. of the product budget] must be formulated clearly, unambiguously and measurably.'[9]

Concepts such as 'comprehensive', 'consistent', 'clear' and 'unambiguous' have a strong 'feel-good' factor: they are attractive and have great communicative power. None the less, sufficient arguments have now been put forward against these 'feel-good' concepts:

- Performance measurement should not be comprehensive but bounded. The same performance may need multiple definitions and quantifications for different functions or forums (Chapter 5).
- Performance measurement must always allow the manager and professional freedom, also for inconsistencies. An example is the necessity of an indirect link between performance and reward. An indirect link means that inconsistency may arise: a single production figure leads to multiple judgements and therefore to multiple rewards (Chapter 5).
- Unambiguity does not work in an ambiguous world. This was illustrated by the example of the definition of academic publication in Chapter 5, where an unambiguous definition was incompatible with the academic world, with its countless specializations, in which multiple meanings are given to 'academic publication'. Ambiguity might be unclear for outsiders, but does do justice to reality.

A counter to comprehensiveness, consistency and unambiguity, as requirements set on a performance measurement system, is the value of variety. When a performance is multiple valued, its measurement must likewise be multiple valued. An organization must therefore always have a certain variety in its measurement systems, as well as tolerating variety within systems.

Variety of systems

In the first place, other systems for forming a judgement may also be used *alongside* a system of output measurement. If there are multiple systems, then professionals have the opportunity to be accountable in multiple ways.

Some examples of measurement systems that may be used alongside performance measurement are:

- peer opinions, which may be solicited to assess the performance of the professionals in several dimensions, such as an external programme review of a research institution (university);

- customer opinions on their satisfaction with the services provided, such as a student questionnaire (university) or a survey of litigants (district court);
- opinions of employees, who may be asked to evaluate their own performance and their satisfaction with the organization's performance, such as surveys among nurses, which can yield interesting information on how surgeons perform;
- opinions of external professionals, which is to say professionals from outside the profession concerned, such as recruiters with respect to the quality of graduates (university) or lawyers with respect to the quality of a judge (district courts).

This kind of variety means for the professional that his or her performance is never assessed by performance measurement exclusively. For the manager it means that his or her policy decisions are never completely dependent on the results of performance measurement. Variety of this kind guards against unilateral judgements, gives freedom to the manager and the professional (which weakens perverse effects) and also does justice to the complexity and multiple-value nature of public products.

Variety within the system

Second, a variety of product definitions and performance indicators can also be tolerated within the performance measurement system. When a professional organization's products are multiple valued, a single product can be defined and measured in multiple ways. A performance measurement system that offers no freedom in this respect is fairly likely to become perverted.

In Chapter 5, I gave the example of the definition of an academic publication. It is common in the university world to distinguish between academic publications (intended for and refereed by peers) and professional publications (intended for a broader public).

Suppose now that a research group is due for assessment and that a ratio has to be provided of the number of scientific publications to the size of the faculty. Variety in this case means providing the freedom to use multiple definitions of 'academic publication' and therefore to produce multiple production figures. Sometimes these definitions will augment each other, and sometimes conflict.

Conclusion: the benefits of variety

In the extreme case there are two opposing models. The model of comprehensiveness and consistency sets out to control an organization's entire products: everything an organization does is defined as a product and product definitions are unambiguous.

Against this there is a model of variety, with multiple systems for measuring performance, and multiple product definitions used in these multiple systems, and with none of the systems pretending to provide a complete picture of reality. Indeed, there may even be some overlap between different product definitions.

Variety has numerous benefits:

* *Fewer incentives for perverse behaviour.* It moderates the incentives for perverse behaviour.[10] The professionals always have freedom: product definitions are not fixed and other systems that measure different aspects of the professional performance are used alongside the performance measurement system.
* *Freedom for the manager.* The freedom the system offers is also attractive for the manager, who is less of a prisoner of the system and is free to set his own priorities, if they deviate from the performance measurement outcomes.
* *Efficiency.* Furthermore, tolerance for variety can also be efficient. It relieves organizations of the burden of integrating and coordinating all the different product definitions.
* *Authoritative outcomes.* A system that tolerates variety leads to authoritative outcomes. One measurement system, without tolerance for variety, implies giving a single-value picture of a multiple-value reality.

  1 If the same results emerge consistently from a measurement system with variety (e.g. performance on x and y is substandard, according to peers, customers and the performance measurement system), then they are harder for the professional and the manager to ignore. Indeed, the same signal comes consistently from different channels, thereby doing justice to the multiple-valued nature of the professional product. A system with variety will therefore be more powerful than one based on comprehensiveness and unambiguity.

  2 If multiple perspectives give a different picture, this is also factual information. If the productivity of a research group is low, but its reputation among external professionals is good, this is a relevant fact. If a research group scores well on product definition

A, but poorly on product definition B, this is also a relevant fact, because it is evident that the assessment depends on the product definition.

Performance measurement as an ideograph

To conclude this section I make another linguistic excursion. As stated above, concepts such as comprehensive, consistent, clear and unambiguous always appear in a good light in managerial and consultancy jargon. In rhetoric, concepts of this kind are referred to as ideographs.[11] Ideographs have three characteristics:

- they represent a collective, prescriptive obligation, implying that everyone is in favour of comprehensiveness, consistency and completeness;
- they provide legitimacy for what are often dubious or harmful phenomena, as when a given policy that is ineffective or inefficient is given legitimacy by appealing to its comprehensiveness, consistency and completeness;
- they are always somewhat ambiguous and have no fixed meaning. Indeed their meaning can vary, which allows the concept to survive forever.

In this and previous chapters I have shown that comprehensiveness and consistency can cause problems in performance measurement. Comprehensive performance measurement is a strong incentive for perverse behaviour. Consistency does no justice to the multiple-valued nature of public products; it is much more attractive to tolerate variety.

However, the rhetorical power of these concepts is strong; they reduce a complex reality to something clear and understandable. Their rhetorical power means that they keep cropping up and causing all manner of negative effects. Because the concepts are somewhat ambiguous, they can survive forever. If comprehensiveness, consistency and completeness are ultimately revealed to be dysfunctional, there will still be some resistance to arguments in favour of performance measurement based on inconsistent product definitions. Ideographs such as comprehensiveness, consistency and completeness are powerful concepts, but are also multi-interpretable. With a little amendment they can continue to do their work. In other words, ideographs hamper an organization's learning process and block the path towards improving performance measurement.

Ideographs are extremely harmful. It is therefore necessary to expose concepts as ideographs, to create freedom for a more intelligent use of performance measurement.

4 Differentiate between types of products: no comprehensive performance measurement

If performance measurement can never be a comprehensive and consistent system, a logical consequence is for an organization to differentiate its products, and then to select the products on which it is to focus. This differentiation can take place based on two criteria: the product's relevance and its nature.

With respect to the *relevance* of a product, it is usual to make a distinction between an organization's daily, routine products and its critical products. Products are critical when they are of strategic importance to, or carry significant risks for, an organization. With respect to the *nature* of products, a distinction may be made from the perspective of performance measurement between:

- *single-value products*: products with an unambiguous definition which are relatively easy to count;
- *multiple-value products*: products that have to meet several conflicting values, and are therefore hard to define unambiguously or to count.

Table 6.2 compares and contrasts the two types of products:

- *Critical and multiple valued.* A management consultancy is a professional organization. If it has to make a recommendation to a major company of great strategic importance to the customer, it is a critical and multiple-value product. It is critical because of the importance of the subject, and multiple valued because the recommendation will be assessed on many criteria: quality, communicability, relevance for the customer and feasibility, as well as numerous quantified criteria, such as turnover, number of consultancy days and result.
- *Critical and single valued.* The marking period for examinations is single valued: there is a date for sitting the examination and a date on which the figures have to be submitted to the educational administration. The figures on marking periods may be critical to a university,

Table 6.2 Differentiation in performance measurement

	Critical	Daily routine
Multiple-value products	A consultancy report to a customer regarding his or her future strategy	Hip replacement line
Single-value products	The marking period for examinations	Telephone access

because failing to mark examinations on time can strongly influence student satisfaction with a degree programme. This satisfaction in turn is an important indicator in university rankings.

- *Daily routine and multiple valued.* Innovation allows certain professional activities to be standardized. What were once complex activities tend to become relatively simple procedures. Consider hip operations, which were once a major surgical and technical feat, whereas hospitals now have 'hip replacement lines', and some hip operations have been standardized. Of course, the operation remains a multiple-value activity, but has none the less become daily routine.
- *Daily routine and single valued.* Countless activities in organizations fall into this category. An example is the maximum number of times that a telephone in a consultancy firm should be allowed to ring before being answered. Or how many months before the start of an academic year that the entire teaching roster is available. These products are relatively simple to measure, and are moreover part of the organizational routine.

One of the lessons of performance measurement is that aiming for comprehensiveness (i.e. that all performance is incorporated into the system) is hardly cost-effective and leads to information overload, which is then not utilized. Once an organization recognizes the differences between its products, a number of strategies become possible for focusing on a limited number of them.

It is surprising how infrequently this happens. Research conducted by Bordewijk and Klaassen in nine large Dutch municipalities revealed that only two of them were able to resist the temptation to expand and perfect the performance measurement system. These two municipalities draw a distinction between types of tasks and declare performance measurement applicable only to well-definable tasks.

The most awkward and least meaningful kind of performance measurement is of critical and multiple-value products. There is therefore much to be said for focusing on the other three types of products.

Focus on single-value products

For the professional, single-value products are often the least interesting, and may therefore become the stepchildren in the organization. This may be why performance measurement should focus on products of this kind. Whereas professional ethos is a guarantee for the quality of multiple-value products, the same is not true of single-value products. Performance measurement with a focus on single-value products has three benefits:

- it respects professional autonomy regarding critical and multiple-value products;
- it focuses on products that receive little professional attention;
- that also lend themselves to performance measurement.

Focus on routines

An organization may also opt to use performance measurement mainly for organizational routines. The reasoning is that the critical products have such a major significance for the organization that they will be a subject of discussion between management and professionals outside the scope of performance measurement, and will also be subject to the disciplining of performance measurement to a smaller extent.

Indirect control of multiple-value products

At least as important is that a focus on single-value products or routines can have positive side-effects on the organization's multiple-value products. The idea then is that the orderly and disciplined creation of single-value and routine products has a disciplining influence on the multiple-value products.

> Performance of services to students at an educational institution, such as the number of examinations marked within the agreed period, or the availability of study material at least x weeks before the start of a course, can be measured. The underlying idea is that a student is entitled to be treated correctly. Performance measurement that embodies this aim compels discipline in creating single-value products. This disciplining may then filter through into multiple-value products. Lecturers who know that a student is being treated correctly and that attention is being given as a matter of course to the demands and life world of students may well adopt a different attitude in their teaching (the multiple-value product).

The impact of performance measurement on multiple-value products is thus shaped in an indirect way, via single-value products or the routines.

Chapter 7

Dynamics

Towards lively performance measurement

1 Introduction

How can performance measurement be a lively activity? A first step is tolerating variety. Anyone who tolerates variety in performance measurement (see Chapter 6) recognizes that one performance may be viewed from multiple perspectives and can therefore have more than one meaning. This will increase the liveliness of performance management.

Performance measurement is only really lively when attention extends beyond products – numbers of convictions, operations, or school leavers with diplomas. This is the second step: there also has to be a focus on the *creation process* of these products – investigating, performing an operation, or teaching.

This chapter first addresses the need to consider both products and processes in forming a judgement on a professional organization's performance, and to combine information intelligently from the two sources (Sections 2 to 4). If an organization succeeds, it may boost the liveliness and dynamism of performance measurement.

The next question is how to play the performance measurement game when both products and processes are being assessed (Section 5).

Section 6 discusses how an organization should deal with new products and product definitions that arise as a result of dynamics inside and outside the organization.

2 Product and process

The differences between performance measurement focused on products and on processes are shown in Table 7.1.[1] I illuminate the differences using a lawcourt as an example. The example may be easily translated to other professional sectors.

Products (output) play a role when a judgement has to be formed on the performance of a court, as do the processes (throughput). Products include

Table 7.1 Performance measurement of products and processes

Product-oriented performance measurement	Process-oriented performance management
Result	Throughput
Low tolerance of more than one criterion	High tolerance of the use of more criteria
Appraisal by an expert	Dialogue between professionals
'Long-distance' methods	'Local' methods
External reviewer	Internal reviewer
Ex-post checks	'Real time' picture
All functions, including sanctions, nouns	Strong accent on learning function, verbs
'Demystification'	Surprise
Mutual trust low	Mutual trust high

the number of rulings or the turnaround time of a case. These items can be captured in the figures. The creation process is far more complicated. How did the court treat the person seeking justice? Was the ruling robust enough to withstand any appeal to a higher court? Does the judgement satisfy the value of legal uniformity? It is conceivable for a court to demonstrate impressive production figures, but for the people seeking justice to feel badly treated because the judges always seem to be in a hurry and many rulings collapse on appeal.

The above leads to the conclusion that *several criteria* may be applicable to judging a professional's performance. Important criteria, besides a production figure and a turnaround time per case, include the treatment of people in the court, the communicability of the ruling, the arguments supporting the ruling, how well the ruling is able to withstand appeal, how the ruling contributes to legal uniformity and so on. A good production figure can be assessed positively, in that it helps reduce turnaround times, and people seeking justice have a shorter time to wait for a ruling. A high production figure can also be assessed negatively, for example if it is detrimental to legal uniformity or if the quality of the supporting legal arguments leaves something to be desired. A product approach has only one criterion: the production figure.

Because many aspects play a role in forming the judgement, it is difficult for an expert to judge the performance based on the production figure alone. In forming a judgement on the court, account must at any rate be taken of the criteria of productivity, treatment, legal quality, turnaround time and legal uniformity. Some conflict may arise between these criteria. A sharp focus on the legal quality of the ruling may substantially lengthen the turnaround time of a case, which is not always in the interest of the people seeking justice. The professionals must therefore always trade these criteria off against each other. This trade-off may moreover vary depending on the branch of law or the type of case, and may change as time passes. For instance, after a period spent focusing on productivity – in order to clear an acute backlog, for example – attention could shift back to quality. For this reason, forming a judgement demands continuous *dialogue between professionals* on the question of what, given the actual situation a court finds itself in, is the best trade-off between the criteria. It is extremely risky for an expert to form a unilateral judgement based on static criteria, always interrelated in the same way, because that would be to ignore the characteristics of the specific situation.

Local considerations and assessment methods are also extremely important. One court is not the same as another. Lawyers in metropolitan areas may be more assertive than their rural counterparts, for example in how procedural law is applied by the court. This aspect may have consequences for productivity. Critical legal professionals will be more likely to cause procedural overruns and so reduce productivity than their more subservient colleagues. Another possible consequence is that 'treatment' of people may be defined differently in metropolitan areas than in rural areas, which in turn may also have consequences for productivity. If attention is given exclusively to productivity figures, 'long-distance' methods will be enough, and the same system may be used for every court. If a reviewer would prefer a richer picture of a court, some tolerance for variety is important, as are local considerations and assessment systems.

In view of the above, an *internal reviewer* will generally be best placed to form a detailed view of the process. If productivity figures have a central position, an external reviewer is sufficient.

Some degree of *surprise* is often involved in a process approach. Any outsider looking into the profession may be astounded by its complexity and richness: dialogue with the professional often reveals his or her 'tacit knowledge', which then leads to a richer dialogue and richer images. Verbs are appropriate in describing a process approach. The reviewer is less interested in numbers of rulings than in administering justice. How does a judge keep his knowledge of rules and case law up to date? How are case files studied? How is the rule applied? How are parties in civil proceedings urged to reach a settlement? How does the judge lead the hearing? Does this contribute to reaching a settlement?

The product approach is based far more on an attitude of *demystification*: the primary process is complex and difficult to grasp, but the measurement of products allows it to be described and understood. The primary process can be reduced to a figure.

The process approach thus leads to a lively and ongoing process, with management and professionals interacting regularly to form pictures of the performance delivered. An internal reviewer is close to the professional process and is therefore far better able to form 'ongoing' and 'real time' pictures of, and to comment on, performance than the external reviewer, who assesses performance *ex post*.

This form of performance measurement can have a positive effect in that the reviewer, manager and professionals learn about the performance, the criteria for the performance and possible improvements. Learning is actually the goal of the process approach. If the focus is on learning, trust may develop between the reviewer and the professionals: trust is a *sine qua non* for the sound operation of the process approach.

3 What professionals are bad at: the perverse effects of the process approach

Anyone opting exclusively for a product approach will in due course be evoking the perverse effects mentioned in Chapter 2. However, a process approach, with its focus on the dialogue between professionals, is not without risk either. Professional organizations or groups may tend to be relatively closed. They have their own values and a specific expertise, which an outsider will find difficult to master. Mintzberg has pointed out the non-intervention principle that is often in evidence in professional organizations.[2] Professionals tend not to intervene in the activities of professional colleagues. The explanation is not surprising: by avoiding interventions, professionals avoid criticism of each other's performance and they acquire additional degrees of freedom, both for themselves and for others. Furthermore, a professional group is often characterized by mutual dependencies. The professionals come into contact with each other everywhere – certainly if organizations and groups are small – and will need each other repeatedly in the future. This can lead to a culture in which people deal cautiously with each other.

Being closed means that self-control and self-monitoring are extremely important, but the non-intervention principle explains why they sometimes lack teeth. The consequence is that professional organizations exhibit both exclusivity and a limited self-healing capacity. This situation calls into question the assumption behind a process approach – that professionals are in a position to arrive at a picture of performance through dialogue. Being closed can have the following consequences for an organization.

Too insensitive to external developments

A closed organization can be too insensitive to external developments that may impose new and different requirements on the profession (e.g. massification processes) – whether in education, health care or the judicial system – and set new requirements for the profession. They may lead to a different trade-off between quality and productivity and raise discussion on existing working methods. One effect may be a tendency to deprofessionalize, as certain activities must and can be standardized.

For instance, for many years the Dutch tax authorities took no action against certain people who refused to pay tax. There was an official guideline to ignore non-payers in certain traveller sites, Hell's Angels' clubhouses, callshops, cannabis nurseries and soft-drug outlets. An attitude of this kind may make sense from the professional perspective (for example, if the costs of additional police presence when collecting taxes outweighs the proceeds). However, social acceptance of the practice may be a completely different story. Political intervention brought an end to this internal practice once it became public knowledge.[3]

Legalistic and defensive response

A closed organization might develop a defensive and reactive attitude: the tendency to defend existing practices with an appeal to prevailing professional values, or a tacitly assumed superiority of practices that have become established among professionals. An example in this connection is Mintzberg's 'pigeonholing', which refers to professionals' fondness for allocating new developments to existing categories.

I mentioned above the example of the heart unit with a high mortality rate at a training hospital in the Netherlands. The first response of staff and management was that figures of that kind meant almost nothing. Training hospitals, they reasoned, accepted patients in a worse state than many normal hospitals and therefore had a higher mortality rate almost by definition. However, a Health Care Inspectorate investigation revealed a totally different reality: poor cooperation between doctors and a sloppy management style. The appeal to the hospital's academic status was a form of defensive and legalistic response: existing working practices were fine, and anyone who thought otherwise did not know what they were talking about. There was insufficient critical reflection on their own working methods.

Externalizing

A closed organization has incentives for externalizing: the explanation for poor performance is sought outside the organization concerned. For example, a university's poor teaching performance may be blamed on falling standards in secondary education, or on the attitude of the new generation of students. Externalizing is a very comfortable pastime, because if you externalize you do not have to change.

If exclusivity as described above exists, a process approach will have significant risks. A process approach is based on interaction between professionals. However, it can degenerate into a dialogue in which the professional is insensitive to external developments, behaves defensively and externalizes problems. A process approach can then be perverse: in the course of time it creates only rationalizations and specious arguments.

Here, too, the view that emerges is mixed. Like quantified performance measurement, the process approach can also have perverse effects. On the other hand, the process approach would appear to be a valuable addition to the product approach. How should these mixed views be reconciled?

4 Besides judging production, judge also the professional process

When a role exists for a process approach alongside performance measurement, the resulting situation is as shown in Table 7.2 and there are four types of possible judgement.

An initial judgement is that a professional's productivity is high (performance measurement) and he or she also does well from a professional perspective (process approach). Some examples would be a researcher who publishes frequently and is also innovative; a hospital that performs many operations in accordance with professional standards; a court that produces many rulings which are always upheld on appeal. In sporting terms, these are the star players: a football player who not only scores many goals but also plays elegantly, is loyal to the team, helps in defence when needed and helps others to improve their game.

A second judgement is that a professional performs poorly from the perspective of productivity. The researcher publishes rarely, the surgeon

Table 7.2 Four types of judgement on performance

	Productivity: high	*Productivity: low*
Professional judgement: good	Star player	Winger
Professional judgement: poor	Bean counter	Degradation candidate

has a high mortality rate and the court rules only sporadically. However, the professional judgement may be positive. The researcher provides inspirational leadership to a young and talented research group, and they enjoy a sparkling international reputation. The surgeon's skills are so outstanding that many of the patients whom he accepts have been written off as untreatable elsewhere, and the judge is given only difficult mega-cases because of his special knowledge and wisdom.

A professional of this kind may be compared with a winger in football. The striker who plays on the wings keeps close to the sidelines but scores few goals himself, certainly for a player in a forward position. However, his game creates opportunities for others – the forward and the midfielders – and he can set the scene for others to score (compare this with the example of the researcher who helps others perform better). This professional is also a winger in another sense: he or she resides on the boundaries of the system, which can make his specific performance difficult to measure. No account is taken of the patient's condition when counting deaths; mega-cases seem few and far between when counting rulings.

A third type of performance is that of the 'bean counter': the professional who does everything in his or her power to score well in the performance measurement system, but does less well from a professional point of view. The researcher publishers frequently, but does so by constantly recycling existing knowledge. The surgeon may produce impressive production figures, but he leaves the difficult cases to others. The judge produces many rulings, but has a poor reputation for rudeness to the parties in the court and the breakneck speed at which he pushes cases through. This is the quadrant occupied by the lazy forward: the player who wants only to score, never helps in defence, even to avoid goals by the other team, never fetches the ball from the midfield, and does not inspire his fellow players, but irritates them with his air of stardom.

Finally, a judgement can be negative from the perspective of both productivity and professionalism. The productivity figure is low, while the professional judgement of performance is also poor. In football terms, this is the degradation candidate.

The figure shows that both judgements – the professional judgement resulting from the process approach and the judgement on productivity that emerges from the performance measurement system – are necessary in forming an accurate view of a professional's performance.

Product and process acquire meaning in relation to each other

The discussion in Section 2 (above) and in Table 7.1 implies that the point here is not choosing either process or product, or that one of the two approaches is superior. It is, rather, that both approaches are used simultaneously and that the tension which arises between them is exploited. Robert Quinn once referred to this as the 'management of competing values'.[4] I first give an example and then develop the idea further.

Example: community policing

Many countries have a system of community policing, in which police officers are given full responsibility for the safety and liveability of a neighbourhood.[5]

At some point, an assistant commissioner has to form a view of a beat officer's performance. The assistant commissioner can use performance measurement as a tool. Has the number of reports of public nuisance gone down? Are there fewer cases of shoplifting? How many tickets were issued, and for which offences? Has any survey been carried out among neighbourhood residents into their satisfaction with police performance? If so, how do the outcomes of the survey compare with earlier surveys?

These figures offer only an extremely limited view of the beat officer's performance. A beat officer's activities are a good match for the characteristics of products and services shown in Table 1.1. The nature of a beat officer's activities is highly relational and he is almost always dependent on the efforts of his co-products. The beat officer makes certain agreements with residents and businesses. He maintains his networks in the community. He observes that certain locations are unsafe and discusses with the municipality what can be done about the situation: he organizes public information activities, makes agreements with schools on scheduling, with shopkeepers' associations on joint patrols and so on. The relationship between his effort and the results cannot therefore be determined. Performance measurement has a limited meaning in activities like this, and if they are applied they usually cause perverse effects.

As an alternative, a process approach is more appropriate, in which the beat officer demonstrates which activities he performs. This process approach may be carried out in a variety of ways. The simplest and most informal form is a tour through the neighbourhood (i.e. a professional inspection): the beat officer can point out his regular contacts, the changes made to buildings or traffic management, that parts of the neighbourhood are safer and in what ways, and how shopkeepers can notify each other of robberies. If the neighbourhood is troubled with rowdy youths, the beat officer can show how much he has invested in good relations with the young people's parents and that there are now fewer hangouts where the youths loiter and more facilities for them.

This process approach gives meaning to production figures. If the nuisance caused by young people is considerable but few tickets are issued, the assistant commissioner may be surprised. However, the production figure is given meaning when the beat officer points out his close contacts with the parents, and how he frequently confronts them with their children's troublesome behaviour. He is evidently a 'winger' in this regard: he has a low production figure, but a good professional performance. Production figures are not meaningless, because the assistant commissioner can use them in asking for clarification from the beat officer. Why is the number of shop break-ins falling? The beat officer can point to the considerable effort he has put into persuading shopkeepers to cooperate in the fight against robberies. The assistant commissioner's judgement may be that the beat officer is a 'star player' in this regard. The production figures show that the level of nuisance at the weekends has fallen sharply. The beat officer reports this fact with some pride. As the assistant commissioner persists with his questioning, the most important explanation turns out to be that the municipality has closed a cinema and the beat officer was not involved in the closure at all. He will have shown himself to be a true 'bean counter' in this respect.

A process approach can be formalized as rules of the game, determining, for example, which subjects are to be discussed, who is to be involved in this discussion, how conclusions will be drawn, which agreements will be made and how their fulfilment can be monitored. The idea is that making explicit rules of the game in this way helps in the systematic exchange and use of knowledge and information.

The essence of the example: switching between product and process

What is the essence of performance measurement as it is embodied in this example? The answer is simple: the assistant commissioner moves constantly back and forth between performance measurement and the process approach. He uses performance measurement to form a sharper picture of the process; the process approach contributes meaning to production figures. Acting in this way has a number of benefits.

First benefit. Performance measurement: no mushrooming

First, the assessor is not solely dependent on performance measurement, which is one-sided. If an assessor relies only on a performance measurement system, and the related perverse effects eventually start to appear, then there is nothing for it but to find a solution within this system. As a result, performance measurement systems become clogged, with problems being solved within the system by patching it up (i.e. additional product definitions and performance indicators). However, the patches applied will also have their perverse effects, so that the system eventually goes off the rails. The system may become so complicated that it loses its controlling effect. The Law of Mushrooming starts to act.

The process approach is an intervention applied from outside the performance measurement system. Figures – however limited their meaning – are used in questioning the professional critically on his or her process. The assistant commissioner does not use the figures to form a judgement, but to ask the beat officer critical questions and so form a detailed picture of the professional performance.

This leads to three conclusions. The first is that production figures are mainly a trigger for forming a view of performance. The second is that the figures acquire meaning only if they are linked to a process approach, which gives attention to the professional judgement of performance. The third is that allowing product and process to interact makes it unnecessary constantly to improve and refine performance measurement.

Second benefit. Process approach: beyond the defensive dialogue

Second, Section 3 points out that a process approach has perverse effects of its own. A process approach can lead to the professional being given the freedom to erect defensive arguments or to externalize conspicuous underperformance. The process approach thus generates professional rationalizations and specious arguments. The assessor may attempt to expose these rationalizations and will succeed in the most favourable cases, but in the worst cases will merely elicit new defensive arguments. The discussion is then fruitless, with no authoritative outcome.

A different picture emerges if use is made of both the process approach and performance measurement. Legalistic arguments put forward by professionals, which may be no more than rationalizations, can then be confronted with the production of those same professionals.

Example: university readers

Alongside products (e.g. the number of Master's degrees), processes also play a role in forming a judgement about a university's teaching performance. Questions on the quality of the study material, the related use of ICT and the relationship between theory and practical material are not raised from the perspective of production, despite their importance in the teaching process. Suppose an assessor who looks at both products and processes observes the messy appearance of the study material. Students are expected to study readers compiled from many separate articles, with little consistency and considerable overlap.

An initial judgement will duly be negative: poorly organized readers, with considerable overlap between the texts, are not beneficial to the learning process and students' results. A process approach implies that lecturers will be questioned on this subject. The dialogue with lecturers may give rise to a completely different picture. Far from being a problem, the lecturers claim that what was seen as poorly organized study material was actually a solution to the new learning style of the latest generation of students. This generation, which grew up with the Internet, has a far greater aptitude for dealing with fragmented information. A reader compiled from separate articles and considerable overlap is consistent with this learning style: the students zap through the reader, never reading any of the texts from beginning to end but still receiving all the information thanks to the overlap. What is more, a traditional book, with its linear argument, is no longer suitable for these students. How should the assessor deal with this information? Is this a well-thought-out educational concept produced by inspired lecturers? Or a rationalization produced by lazy professionals?

Performance measurement may play a role in giving meaning to this picture. Suppose performance measurement reveals poor student progress, with an extremely low pass rate. On the other hand, the figures for courses that use traditional study material are far better. This may be a reason to go back to the lecturers and question them again about their attitudes to learning styles. If other performance measurement then reveals that the lecturers concerned spend many hours on research and few on teaching, the use of both performance measurement systems will have led to the following dynamic picture:

- The first observation was of sloppy and fragmented teaching material.
- The dialogue with the lecturers turned this picture around completely: fragmented teaching material is just what the modern student needs, and the teaching material had been carefully compiled in line with a well-thought-out teaching philosophy.
- Then came the performance measurement, revealing a low pass rate and students spending far too many years at university, coupled with insufficient time spent by lecturers on teaching.
- The picture then took another about turn: the teaching philosophy was not well-thought-out, but the learning style of the modern student was merely being used as an excuse for sloppy and careless teaching.
- This dynamic switching from one performance measurement system to the other continues, and may ultimately lead to a more subtle picture in which some lecturers have developed the teaching philosophy honestly and are also

achieving good results, while other lecturers use the teaching philosophy to give legitimacy to sloppy behaviour. The judgement on these two types of lecturer is clear. Yet another group of lecturers also developed the teaching material honestly but without achieving good results. Judgement of this group of lecturers should possibly be postponed, and management and professionals should consider how they can learn more about modern students and how they should be taught.

The above list leads to three conclusions. The first is that a process approach may be an incentive to produce rationalizations. The second conclusion is that these rationalizations can be exposed using the results of performance measurement. The third conclusion is that a process approach can be given meaning by linking it with performance measurement. Allowing product and process to interact prevents the process approach from degenerating into an endless debate between the manager and the professional.

Freedom for the game

The use of the two approaches gives the assessor a chance to play the performance measurement game. The professional presents a view of the process, which can be subjected to critical questioning by the assessor using performance measurement.

The professional can also improve his or her game. If performance measurement leads to a poor assessment, he or she can use the process approach to show that everything possible has been done to avoid these figures. The use of the two approaches gives both parties *freedom* to play the game and not to be dependent on one approach.

The use of production figures may have three functions in this game:

- The figures may *confirm* the picture that emerges from the process approach, where high production coincides with good professional performance (star player) or low production coincides with poor professional performance (degradation candidate).
- The figures may *expose* the truth about the picture that emerges from the process approach, where the assessor confronts the professional's claims of good professional performance with figures, and the result of the dialogue is that a good professional performance was not delivered.
- The figures may *add fine detail* to the picture that emerges from a process approach, as when a reduction in public nuisance may be partly

attributed to the closure of a cinema (see the community policing example above).

Again: the boundary spanner

An organization wishing to use both approaches and to compare them critically with each other will need to identify the eligible players.

As in Chapter 5, the question again is where in the organization can the 'boundary spanner' between the managerial system (where the product approach will often dominate) and the professional system (where a process approach will often dominate) be found. The operation of a performance measurement system will depend strongly on this boundary spanner – the managing professional. Without this boundary spanner it is very likely that the product orientation will displace the process orientation, or vice versa.

On the one hand, the boundary spanner has to be close enough to the primary process to be able to use the process approach. On the other hand, he or she must also be sufficiently remote from the primary process to be able to examine it critically without succumbing to pitfalls such as the non-interference principle. On the one hand, the boundary spanner resides in the managerial system to help convey the necessity for reporting on an organization's performance. On the other hand, he or she often resides sufficiently far away from the managerial system to be able to put the meaning of performance measurement into perspective.

5 Transform a defensive discussion on past performance into a pro-active discussion on future performance

An important assumption in the argument outlined in Section 4 (above) is that the professional adopts a cooperative attitude when performance measurement is robust. He or she is challenged by the game of performance measurement and the process approach, and is willing to play the game. It goes without saying that this does not always happen. A professional who sets out to conceal poor performance has a strong incentive not to play this game of performance measurement and the process approach.

There is then a risk of conflict arising between the professional and the manager on the delivered performance, in which one party relies on the quantified performance and the other party on the process approach. The literature on network organizations always warns about conflicts of this type.[6] A conflict between mutually dependent parties which takes place in a single spectrum (in this case: product versus process) has no winners. Even if one of the parties manages to impose his or her own view, the future relationship with the loser can suffer so much harm that the winner also becomes a loser. An important question that arises is how to avoid the game between the manager and the professional becoming one-dimensional.

The necessity of a multi-dimensional playing field

One answer to this question is that it is important to create a multi-dimensional playing field. For example, this may be achieved by not being restricted to the product–process dimension, but also using the *ex post/* justification–*ex ante*/learning dimension.

If a playing field of this kind exists, both the manager and the professional are given freedom to manoeuvre and therefore to avoid deadlock, with the manager relying on products and the professional on processes.

- A deadlock may arise if a manager observes low production at a professional unit, while the unit concerned puts up process-related arguments (considerable innovation at the expense of production; caution a priority over production: see the examples of the professor and the court in this chapter).
- Both the manager and the professional can persist in developing their arguments without arriving at a joint view. The manager observes that other, comparable professional units are also innovating, without production suffering. The professional responds that his or her own process differs in several respects from these other units, rendering comparison impossible. In a later round even more new arguments will be raised, but no fruitful discussion will result.
- This discussion focuses on the past, which will only exacerbate the deadlock. After all, the past cannot be changed: the production has been delivered, the process defined.
- A manager who believes that these arguments have an element of rationalization would be well advised to halt the debate about the past at some point and to invite the professional to reach agreement about the future. A defensive discussion of past performance can then be converted into a pro-active discussion of future performance. The professor with his or her innovative research can be invited to say when production may be expected (product).

- If the professor says production is unlikely, the future development of this research may be discussed in the presence of the fellow professional mentioned, who is evidently capable of production (process). An intervention by a third party of this kind, with discussion not about the past but about the future, may be useful. The manager may then invite this third party to identify opportunities for raising production. The fellow professional is not then placed in the role of assessor – which could lead to non-intervention – but of professional adviser. If the fellow professional can identify opportunities for improvement, it will be hard for the professor to ignore these views. Here too, a defensive discussion about the past is converted into a pro-active discussion about the future. A manager who observes that other professionals are also innovating, without production suffering, can attempt to translate this observation into agreements about the future, as opposed to conducting a debate about the past.
- This translation can enhance the professional's commitment to improving production, or, if no such improvement is possible, can produce a more accurate judgement of the process. This commitment simplifies judgement in a later round.

6 Provide freedom for new performance, new products and new systems, but in moderation

A system of product definitions always provides a temporary view of an organization's products. Both *internal* and *external* dynamics cause an organization's products to develop. If performance measurement is to be robust, the performance measurement system must adapt to this dynamic situation.

Internal and external dynamics

Every performance measurement system has a temporary life span: performance measurement becomes exhausted in the course of time.[7] This may have a negative explanation: the professional learns how to optimize his or her behaviour in a given performance measurement system, thus perverting that system (see Chapters 2 and 3). The design principles discussed in Part II of this book can help to make performance measurement more trustworthy, substantial and vital, but at some point the performance measurement system will be exhausted. There may also be a positive explanation: the point is reached when performance measurement has served its purpose well enough and is no longer useful.

Suppose that the Board of an educational institution is dissatisfied with the length of time students are taking for their studies. Students need more than three years on average to complete a two-year Master's degree programme. The final project in particular is prolonged due to the noncommittal way the students are supervised. In response, the Board decides to base funding on the number of Master's degrees awarded. Every Master's degree is worth a given amount, with the amount falling as students take longer over their studies. This performance indicator will be exhausted after a number of years. Following an initial rise, the number of Master's degrees stabilizes (there is evidently no more room for improvement). The performance indicator was once a performance incentive, but has since degenerated into a reporting mechanism for bookkeeping purposes. Every performance indicator has this life span, and is an invitation to identify different indicators.

This is the internal dynamics of performance measurement. There are also *external dynamics*: the environment in which an organization operates changes, demanding a new or different performance measurement.

A ministry has an administration agency that alerts businesses to grants that are available for certain areas of technology. The consultants employed by this administration agency visit different companies in the course of their work. The administration agency submits various production figures to the ministry each year, including a figure representing the ratio of the number of grant applications to the number of company visits. This figure develops poorly as the years pass: the number of company visits for a single application is rising sharply. The explanation is that the administration agency's environment has changed: other public authorities now also grant subsidies for the areas of technology concerned. The consultants have duly modified their strategy: they now identify eligible projects within companies and then determine which public authorities may be approached for these projects. As a guideline, they first investigate which European funds are available, then which funds the other ministries make available, and finally which funds are made available by local and regional public authorities. Only if none of these public authorities has a suitable grant scheme do they investigate which subsidies their own ministry provides. The introduction of this strategy has resulted in an increase in the number of grant applications per company visit, but a fall in the number of grant applications to the ministry concerned per company visit. The environment has changed, the enterprising professional has responded properly, but the performance measurement system is still measuring the old performance.

Dynamics and the need for stability

In these and similar situations, performance measurement creates inertia: it resists moving with the dynamics of product development. One consequence may be that performance measurement impedes innovation, or – if they do indeed innovate – professionals feel underrated. They are innovative, but are unable to make this visible in figures, and are not judged on their innovation. I make a distinction here between three types of innovation of performance management systems.

There is always an element of tension in innovation, as mentioned several times above. On the one hand, a system has to be flexible: it needs to adapt to changed circumstances. On the other hand, if it is to fulfil its intended functions, a system has to be sufficiently stable. Functions such as benchmarking, assessing and judging are more difficult to fulfil if a system is in constant flux. The rules of the game should therefore serve both the interest of innovation and the interest of stability.

First order: new products

First-order change is when new products are created, or when an organization (management or professional) needs to make existing products visible by means of new definitions.

The associated rule of the game is that management and the professional must be given an opportunity to identify new products and make them visible. Both may have an interest in doing so: the manager possibly because his or her environment is demanding a different type of reporting; the professional because innovations in the primary process have created new products.

The need for stability can be served by a rule of the game which says that new products are admitted to a performance measurement system only when they have proven functionality. A manager or professional wishing to introduce a new product is given the freedom outside the existing performance measurement:

- to define new products;
- to state the implications for the existing product definitions;
- to identify associated performance indicators;
- to supply production figures for the new products;
- to indicate the influence of those production figures on the existing production.

If these new products later prove to be effective, they may lead to a change in the portfolio and be given a place in the performance measurement system.

A rule of the game of this kind prevents simplistic criticism of the existing system. Management and professional are forced to specify the new products accurately. When the functionality of the new product definition is proven, it can be incorporated into the existing performance measurement system, thus protecting the system's integrity: it is not burdened with product definitions that have yet to prove their right to exist or have no clear relationship with existing products.

Second and third order: new systems

A performance measurement system might create inertia: not because new products have emerged, but because the performance measurement system itself has become obsolete. The manager or the professional may observe that performance measurement creates too many perverse effects and that it is in the last phase of its life cycle.

The outcome of a reflection on the system's life cycle can be to abandon a performance measurement system – a third-order change. However, the importance of stability applies here too, and relinquishing output control – in favour of input or throughput control – can have significant disadvantages:

- It yields transformation costs. It was stated above that introduction of a performance measurement system has a long turnaround time. If a system of this kind is abandoned and then followed by the introduction of a new system, a long transformation period will ensue, with the associated costs.
- Possible positive effects of performance measurement are no longer gained.
- Input and throughput control have significant disadvantages and negative effects (see Chapter 1). Managing on input leads to a claim culture. Managing on throughput leads to a billing culture.

Stability is therefore also of value. What is the rule of the game from the perspective of stability? The idea is that a second-order change does not imply abandoning a performance measurement system, but changing the position of performance management relative to input and throughput systems.

An important argument for this second-order change is that performance measurement also has a function as a countervailing power for input and throughput systems, which also have their perverse effects – they may lead to a claim or a billing culture. In other words, every system has its dysfunctions and therefore needs the other systems when the dysfunctions are too strong. If, for example, professionals develop an attitude of claiming funds, information on their actual performance might be very helpful for a manager. The idea that systems, whether input-, throughput- or output-oriented, require countervailing systems in order to be effective was also discussed in Chapter 6: performance measurement must always exist alongside other systems of judgement. The more comprehensive the performance measurement system and the less room for other systems, the stronger the perverse effect. This applies *mutatis mutandis* to the alternatives for performance measurement: if they are given too much room, they pervert.

From the perspective of dynamism, a second-order change is somewhat paradoxical. When management and the professional arrive at the conclusion that a performance measurement system has become exhausted, it does not lead to the system being abandoned, but to a change in its relative position. For example, it may temporarily assume a peripheral position, with a more dominant position of input and throughput systems, but it can always return to a more central one.

The dynamics of performance measurement is therefore maintained here too by playing with competing values. Performance measurement is set against input and throughput control, and this tension must be exploited. This is why a more radical, third-order change is not without risk. This playing with competing values is the central message of this chapter. Performance measurement is enlivened by utilizing the tension between product and process, between the performance *ex post* and the performance *ex ante*, and between output, input and throughput systems.

Part III

Chapter 8

Conclusions and three paradoxes

I Conclusions

What should the final conclusion be about performance measurement? Let me summarize the argument of this book:

- Performance measurement has unmistakable positive effects. The idea that output figures cannot play any significant role in forming an image of professional performance is too simple.
- Performance measurement also produces perverse effects. It takes very limited account of the complexity of the profession. Those who nevertheless introduce a system of performance measurement create incentives for these perverse effects.
- At least as important is the dynamic of performance measurement. When performance measurement has a high impact, the Law of Decreasing Effectiveness will start to operate: the higher the impact, the stronger the incentives for perverting behaviour and the smaller the chance of positive effects. Once this law operates, other laws may also be activated, namely Mushrooming and Collective Blindness.
- Perverted systems appear to be resistant. Although they are harmful from a professional perspective, they survive, for example because these systems have external owners. In addition, politicians will pay less and less attention to systems of this kind. While introducing performance measurement may be a sign of political determination, abolishing performance measurement tends to be a political dissatisfier.
- This analysis prompts the conclusion that performance measurement may pervert the profession. The reason for this is not so much the introduction of a system of performance measurement as the impact of such a system. The higher the impact, the more perverse the effects. Consequently, an important question is how to mitigate performance measurement. How can we shape performance measurement so as to

make it meaningful for both professionals and managers? It can be shaped along three lines.

• Effective performance measurement requires interaction, which creates the confidence of managers and professionals in each other and in the system. This interaction may, for example, relate to the functions and forums of output figures: What are the aims of performance measurement and for whom are the output figures meant? (See also Chapter 5.)

• Effective performance measurement requires a tolerance for variety. Variety makes a system richer for professionals and prevents performance measurement from degenerating into an accounting mechanism for rewarding or punishing them. Tolerance for variety may also mean that conflicting product definitions are possible and that there is no monopoly on interpretation. (See also Chapter 6.)

• Effective performance measurement requires attention to be paid to the dynamics: How does performance measurement become a lively activity? The answer to this question is twofold. In addition to attention being paid to a product approach, attention should also be paid to the process of creating a product or service. Furthermore, a system should be able to adapt itself to a changed professional or managerial reality, at least to some extent. (See also Chapter 7.)

• How does one realize the need for interaction, variety and dynamics in practice? By agreeing a number of rules of the game on how to use performance measurement. These rules make the way managers and professionals use performance measurement predictable and mitigate its impact. Table 8.1 summarizes the main rules of the game.

• These rules of the game may be self-evident to readers who have familiarized themselves with this book's line of argument, which has given a great deal of attention to professional values. However, the second column of Table 8.1 lists a number of model or system values: values that are important from the perspective of the system of performance measurement. Each and any of the rules of the game are inconsistent with these values.

The language in the second column of Table 8.1 is very strong and has a cogent logic, which is difficult to contest. However, those who press the mould of the system logic on to the profession will always fail to take the complexity of that profession into account and will therefore cause the perverse effects. This book has frequently illustrated this complexity: professions tend to be multiple value, have great variety and require tolerance for ambiguity. What is a solution in the system logic – integrality, punishing–rewarding and consistency – is exactly the problem in the world of professionals. The force of the system language implies, however, that there are constant incentives to develop integral and consistent systems.

Table 8.1 Rules of the game for performance measurement

Rules of the game for performance measurement	System logic
Limit the number of functions and forums of performance measurement	
Do not change functions and forums unilaterally	Integral performance measurement
Differentiate by type of product and limit the scope of performance measurement	
Limit the impact of performance measurement	
There should be no direct relationship between output and high impact	Performance measurement serves to reward or punish professionals for their performance
Monitoring is an interactive process, also aimed at learning	
In addition to the appraisal of output, an appraisal of processes is necessary; these appraisals may conflict	
Offer room for interpretation from several perspectives	
Offer room for a decentralized incentive structure, even when it deviates from the central incentive structure	Performance measurement systems should be consistent and uniform
Tolerate a variety of product definitions, even when they contradict each other	
Leave room for changes to the system	

2 Paradoxes

The above may also be summarized in another way. When performance measurement is on the interface between the complexity of the profession on the one hand and the unambiguity of the system logic on the other hand, performance measurement will always have a number of paradoxical features. Each of the three types of system logic in Table 8.1 creates a paradox. These paradoxes will only be meaningful to professionals and managers if a concrete system of performance measurement is able to handle them.

- *Paradox 1: The more integral the system of performance measurement, the less effective it will be. Offer room to escape from a system's consequences.* An integral performance measurement system involves the entire performances of an organization and may be applied for all conceivable purposes and functions. The more purposes a system should serve – internal management *and* external accountability; comparing *and* appraising; intended for media *and* fellow-professionals *and* inspectorates – the greater the risk that it will pervert or bureaucratize. Professionals become the prisoners of the system, whereas the system should offer them room for manoeuvre, for example, by confining itself to a particular performance, a number of functions or a number of forums.

- *Paradox 2: The more a system is used to form a judgement, the less effective it will be. Use other appraising mechanisms; limit the scope of performance measurement.* Judgements nearly always have a high impact for professionals and may therefore create incentives for perverting behaviour. Using performance measurement in combination with other appraising mechanisms that are conflicting at first sight will strengthen it. In addition to product-based appraisal, process-based appraisal is desirable. In addition to paying attention to output, attention should be paid to input and throughput. Although these conflicting appraising mechanisms may result in conflicting judgements, they strengthen performance measurement. Any conflict between an output-based judgement and a process-based judgement should be made explicit. If this is impossible, the professionals will be the prisoners of the system and incentives for perversion and bureaucratization will evolve.

- *Paradox 3: The more a system is based on the principles of consistency and uniformity, the less effective it will be. Offer room for variety.* Although the values of consistency and uniformity are understandable from a system perspective, professions are characterized by complexity and variety. Any system that fails to offer room for them will create incentives for perversion and bureaucratization. Tolerating variety will render a system more tailor-made and authoritative for professionals.

As I observed earlier, the system logic is strong. I hope this book has made clear that there is also a professional logic. In a first-generation design of a system of performance measurement, the system logic is likely to dominate. In a first design, for example, products have to be defined and the initial effort will be aimed at doing this as consistently as possible. In a second generation of designs, however, it is important to offer room for professional logic as well, for example, by investing in the rules of the game for interaction between managers and professionals, thus enabling performance measurement to be a meaningful activity rather than to degenerate into bureaucracy and ritual.

Notes

I An introduction to performance measurement

1 For example, P. van der Knaap, 'Resultaatgerichte verantwoordelijkheid', *Bestuurskunde*, The Hague: Elsevier, 2000, no. 5, pp. 237–247.

2 David Osborne and Ted Gaebler, *Reinventing Government*, Reading, MA: Penguin, 1992; David Osborne and Peter Plastrik, *The Reinventor's Fieldbook. Tools for Transforming Your Government*, San Francisco, CA: Jossey Bass, 2000; Geert Bouckaert and Tom Auwers, *Prestaties meten in de overheid*, Bruges: Die Keure, 1999; Christopher Pollitt, *The Essential Public Manager*, Maidenhead: Open University Press, 2003; George A. Boyne *et al.*, *Evaluating Public Management Reforms*, Buckingham: Open University Press, 2003; Tony Bovaird and Elke Löffler, *Public Management and Governance*, Londen: Routledge, 2003; H. Thomas Johnson, *Relevance Lost. The Rise and Fall of Managament Accounting*, Boston, MA: Harvard Business School Press, 1991. I also refer to three scientific journals with a great many articles about performance measurement: *Accounting, Auditing and Accountability Journal*; *Managerial Auditing Journal*; *Public Productivity and Management Review*. For international comparisons see the PUMA (Public Management) activities of the OECD (http://www.oecd.org/puma/).

3 Particularly in many general management handbooks; for example, in David Boddy and Robert Paton, *Management. An Introduction*, London: Prentice Hall, 1998, p. 65.

4 Robert D. Behn and Peter A. Kant, 'Strategies for avoiding the pitfalls of performance contracting', *Public Productivity and Management Review*, 1999, vol. 22, no. 4, pp. 470–489.

5 See, for example, G. Frerks, 'Performance measurement in foreign policy: security policy, proper governance, conflict prevention and human rights', *Towards Result-oriented Accountability*, The Hague: Ministry of Foreign Affairs, 2000, pp. 17–24 (in Dutch).

6 C.N. Parkinson, *Parkinsons's Law*, New York: Penguin, 1964.

7 David Osborne and Ted Gaebler, *Reinventing Government*, Reading, MA: Penguin, 1992, pp. 147–150.

8 David Osborne and Ted Gaebler, op.cit., p. 146.

9 David Osborne and Ted Gaebler, op.cit., pp. 138–139.

10 Delft University of Technology, *An Evaluation of the Use of the University Allocation Model 1996–1999*, Delft: Delft University of Technology (DUT), 2000 (in Dutch).

11 David Osborne and Peter Plastrik, *Banishing Bureaucracy*, Reading, MA: Penguin, 1997, p. 145.

12 R.J. in 't Veld, *Relations Between the State and Higher Education*, The Hague: Kluwer Law International, 1996, pp. 79–80.

13 H. Mintzberg, *Structures in Fives: Designing Effective Organizations*, Princeton, NJ: Prentice-Hall, 1983.

14 M.H. Moore and A.A. Braga, 'Measuring and improving police performance: the lessons of compstat and its progeny', *Policing: An International Journal of Police Strategies and Management*, 2003, vol. 26, no. 3, pp. 439–453.

15 G. Frerks, 'Performance measurement in foreign policy: security policy, proper governance, conflict prevention and human rights', in *Towards Result-oriented Accountability*, Ministry of Foreign Affairs, The Hague 2000, p. 21 (in Dutch); also A.G. Dijkstra, 'Performance measurement in foreign aid', in *Beleidsanalyse* (2000), pp. 13–19 (in Dutch).

2 The perverse effects of performance measurement

1 See David Osborne and Ted Gaebler, *Reinventing Government*, Reading, MA: Penguin, 1992, Appendix B; David Osborne and Peter Plastrik, *The Reinventor's Fieldbook. Tools for Transforming Your Government*, San Francisco, CA: Jossey Bass, 2000.

2 Allard Hoogland, 'Het OM in de beklaagdenbank', *Hollands Maandblad*, 1998, no. 2.

3 James Q. Wilson, *Bureaucracy: What Government Agencies Do and Why They Do It*, New York: Basic Books, 2000.

4 J.A. Winston, on www.city.grande-prairie.ab.ca/perfm_a.htm#Top.

5 For perverse effects of performance measurement in health care see Maria Goddard, 'Enhancing performance in health care: a theoretical perspective on agency and the role of information', *Health Economics*, 2000, vol. 9, pp. 95–107. Furthermore, see, for examples of strategic behavior: Christopher Pollitt, *The Essential Public Manager*, Maidenhead: Open University Press, 2003; George A. Boyne *et al.*, *Evaluating Public Management Reforms*, Buckingham: Open University Press, 2003; Tony Bovaird and Elke Löffler, *Public Management and Governance*, Londen: Routledge, 2003.

6 Robert D. Behn and Peter A. Kant, 'Strategies for avoiding the pitfalls of performance contracting', *Public Productivity and Management Review*, 1999, vol. 22, no. 4, pp. 470–489; P. Smith, 'Outcome-related performance indicators and organizational control in the public sector', *British Journal of Management*, 1993, vol. 4, pp. 135–151.

7 This is an often heard objection to performance measurement within universities; see, for example, a debate in the *Academische Boekengids* 2000 and 2001, nos 23–26.

8 Nancy Zollers and A.K. Ramanathan, 'For-profit charter schools and students disabilities: the sordid side of the business of schooling', *Phi Delta Kappan*, December 1998, vol. 81, pp. 297ff.; Thomas A. Good and Jennifer S. Braden,

The Great School Debate: Choice, Vouchers, and Charters, Englewood Cliffs, NJ: Laurence Erlbaum, 1999.

9 John F. Witte, *The Market Approach to Education: An Analysis of America's First Voucher Program*, Princeton, NJ: Princeton University Press, 2000.

10 Jeroen Trommelen, 'Negentig procent moet dood', *de Volkskrant*, 8 February 2001, p. 13.

11 H.G. Sol, 'Aggregating data for decision support', *Decision Support Systems*, 1985, vol. 1, no. 2, pp. 111–121.

12 Example found in a short article by John J. Videler, 'De domme willekeur van het beoordelingssysteem', *Academische Boekengids*, 2001, p. 16.

13 Mary Bowerman and Shirley Hawksworth, 'Local government internal auditors' perceptions of the Audit Commission', *Managerial Auditing Journal*, 1999, vol. 14, no. 8, pp. 396–407.

14 This is no different in the private sector of course. As a product, a jar of peanut butter is a trade-off between, for example, economic, ecological and safety considerations.

15 Garry D. Carnegie and Peter W. Wolnizer, 'Enabling accountability in museums', *Accounting, Auditing and Accountability Journal*, 1996, no. 5, pp. 84–99.

16 For this mechanism see, for example, Coen Teulings, *Privatisering in het tijdsgewricht van recollectivisering*, Rotterdam: OCFEB, 2000.

17 Anthony L. Iaquito, 'Can winners be losers? The case of the Deming prize for quality and performance among large Japanese manufacturing firms', *Managerial Auditing Journal*, 1999, vol. 14, nos 1/2, pp. 28–35.

18 Edward B. Fiske and Helen F. Ladd, *When Schools Compete. A Cautionary Tale*, Washington, DC: The Brooking Institution, 2000.

19 From F.L. Leeuw, 'Performance auditing, new public management and performance improvement: questions and answers', *Accounting, Auditing and Accountability Journal*, 1996, vol. 9, no. 2, pp. 92–102; F.L. Leeuw, 'Onbedoelde neveneffecten van outputsturing, controle en toezicht?', *Raad voor Maatschappelijke Ontwikkeling, Aansprekend burgerschap*, The Hague: RMO, 2000, pp. 149–171.

20 Ibid.

21 J. Riddertrale and K. Nordstrom, *Karaoke Capitalism*, Harlow: Pearson Education, 2004.

22 P. Bordewijk and H.L Klaasen, *Don't Think You Can Measure Us*, The Hague: VNG uitgevers, 2000, pp. 97–98.

3 The dynamics of performance measurement: five laws

1 A. Visser, *Schoolprestaties belicht*, Groningen: Groningen University, 2003.

2 Ibid., pp. 12–18.

3 Ibid., p. 77.

4 Ibid., pp. 197ff.

5 Ibid., pp. 207–209.

6 For example, in David Osborne and Peter Plastrik, *The Reinventor's Fieldbook. Tools for Transforming Your Government*, San Francisco, CA: Jossey Bass, 2000, pp. 223ff.

7 David Osborne and Peter Plastrik, *Banishing Bureaucracy*, Reading, MA: Penguin, 1997.

8 Philippe d'Iribarne, *La logique de l'honneur – Gestion d'enterprises et traditions nationales*, Paris: Editions du Seuil, 1989.

9 David Osborne and Ted Gaebler, *Reinventing Government*, Reading, MA: Penguin, 1992.

10 The somewhat unfortunate Dutch translation used is 'technische functie'.

11 Geert Boeckaert and Ton Auwers, *Measuring Performance in Government*, Bruges: Die Keure, 1999, p. 38.

12 See also Carol Propper and Deborah Wilson, 'The use and usefulness of performance measures in the public sector', *CMPO Working Paper Series*, Bristol, 2003, no. 03/073, p. 14.

13 P. Smith, 'Outcome-related performance indicators and organizational control in the Public Sector', in Jacky Holloway, Jenny Lewis and Geoff Mallory (eds), *Performance Measurement and Evaluation*, 1995.

14 The description of the Shell case is based upon Heleen de Graaf and Tom Jan Meeus, *Dossier Shell*, www.nrc.nl/dossiers/shell, visited June 2006.

15 Quote from NRC Handelsblad, 23 June 2004, http://www.nrc.nl/dossiers/shell/achtergrond_analyse/article80548.ece, visited June 2006.

16 *Frequently Requested Accounting and Financial Reporting Interpretations and Guidance*, 31 March 2001.

17 Quote from *NRC Handelsblad*, 23 June 2004, http://www.nrc.nl/dossiers/shell/achtergrond_analyse/article80548.ece, visited June 2006.

18 Quote from *NRC Handelsblad*, 23 June 2004, http://www.nrc.nl/dossiers/shell/achtergrond_analyse/article80548.ece, visited June 2006.

19 R.J. in 't Veld, *Relations Between the State and Higher Education*, The Hague: Kluwer Law International, 2001.

20 Andrea M. Serban and Joseph C. Burke, 'Meeting the performance challenge. A nine-state comparative analysis', *Public Productivity and Management Review*, 1998, no. 2, pp. 157–177.

21 Aimee Franklin, 'Managing for results in Arizona, a fifth-year report card', *Public Productivity and Management Review*, 1999, pp. 194–209.

22 Hans Broere, *Symbol City*, The Hague: Netherlands School of Public Administration (NSOB), 2001.

23 'Determined challengers keep heat on the elite', *The Times Higher Education Supplement*, 28 October 2005, p. 2.

24 Ibid.

25 Ibid.

5 Trust and interaction

1 See e.g. P. Smith, 'On the unintended consequences of publishing performance data in the public sector', *International Journal of Public Administration*, 1995, no. 18, pp. 277–310; also R. Kravchuk and R. Schrack, 'Designing effective performance measurement systems', *Public Administration Review*, 1996, vol. 56, no. 4, pp. 348–358.

2 A.G.J. Haselbekke, H.L. Klaassen, A.P. Ros and R.J. in 't Veld, *Counting Performance. Indicators as a Tool for A (More) Efficient Management of Decentralized Governments* (in Dutch), The Hague: VNG, 1990, pp. 131–132.

3 Javier Martinez, *Assessing Quality, Outcome and Performance Management*, Geneva: WHO, 2001; and M. Armstrong and A. Baron, *Performance Management – The New Realities*, London: Chartered Institute of Personnel and Development, 1998.
4 As suggested by Peter C. Smith, 'Performance management in British health care: will it deliver', *Performance Management*, May/June 2002, pp. 103–115.
5 David Osborne and Ted Gaebler, *Reinventing Government*, Reading, MA: Penguin, 1992, Appendix B.
6 *NRC Handelsblad*, 25 September 1996.

6 Content and variety

1 Bobbie Jacobson, 'Hospital mortality league tables', *BMJ*, 2003, no. 326, pp. 777–778.
2 See, for example, ibid.
3 R. Klein and N. Carter, 'Performance measurement: a review of concepts and issues', in D. Beeton (ed.), *Performance Measurement. Getting the Concepts Right*, London: Public Finance Foundation, 1988.
4 See, for example, K.A. Van Peursem, M.J. Pratt and S.R. Lawrence, 'Health management performance. A review of measures and indicators', *Accounting, Auditing and Accountability Journal*, 1995, no. 5, pp. 34–70.
5 Robin T. Lakoff, *The Language War*, Berkeley: University of California Press, 2000.
6 Boje Larsen, 'One measurement is better than 1,000 opinions: is it?', *Managerial Auditing Journal*, 2001, no. 2, pp. 63–68.
7 See coverage in Dutch newspapers, April–May 2006.
8 After P. Bordewijk and H.L. Klaasen, *Don't Think You Can Measure Us*, The Hague: VNG uitgevers, 2000, p. 45.
9 Ibid., p. 93.
10 Carol Propper and Deborah Wilson, 'The use and usefulness of performance measures in the public sector', *CMPO Working Paper Series*, no. 03/073, Bristol, 2003, p. 14.
11 Derived from Rein de Wilde, *De voorspellers. Een kritiek op de toekomstindustrie*, Amsterdam: De Balie, 2000, p. 128.

7 Dynamics: towards lively performance measurement

1 Adapted from Michael Power, 'The audit explosion', in G. Mulgan (ed.), *Life after Politics*, London: Fontana, 1997, pp. 286–293. Similar categorizations may be found in, among other articles, Malcolm Smith *et al.*, 'Structure versus appraisal in the audit process: a test of Kinney's classification', *Managerial Auditing Journal*, 2001, vol. 16, no. 1, pp. 40–49 (Smith discusses the distinction between structure and judgement); also Lai Hong Chung *et al.*, 'The influence of subsidiary context and head office strategic management style on control of MNCs: the experience in Australia', *Accounting, Auditing and Accountability Journal*, 2000, vol. 13, no. 5, pp. 647–668 (Chung discusses the distinction between output and behavioural control); see also Javier Martinez, *Assessing Quality, Outcome and Performance Management*, Geneva: WHO, 2001, and M. Armstrong and

A. Baron, *Performance Management – The New Realities*, London: Chartered Institute of Personnel and Development, 1998.

2 H. Mintzberg, *Structures in Fives: Designing Effective Organizations*, Englewood Cliffs, NJ: Prentice-Hall, 1983.

3 Letter from the State Secretary of Finance to the President of the Lower House of the States General, The Hague, 3 June 2004, ref. DGB2004-3005.

4 Robert Quinn, *Beyond Rational Management*, San Francisco, CA: Wiley, 1998.

5 William M. Rohe, Richard E. Adams and Thomas A. Arcury, 'Community policing and planning', *Journal of the American Planning Assocation*, 2001, vol. 67, no. 1, pp. 51–52.

6 Hans de Bruijn and Ernst ten Heuvelhof, *Networks and Decision Making*, Utrecht: Lemma, 2000.

7 R.J. in 't Veld, *Relations between the State and Higher Education*, The Hague: Kluwer Law International, 2001.

Index

Page numbers in *italic* denote references to figures/tables.